A.A. Custer

Creating the Enemy

Propaganda, Politics, and Public Perception

"The Art of Influence Through Enemy Narratives"

Table of Contents

Creating the Enemy: Propaganda, Politics, and Public Perception 1
Dedication 3
Copyright © 2024 by A.A. Castor 4
Why I Am Writing This Book 5
Warning and Disclaimer 8
About the Author 10
Introduction: Understanding the Role of Enemies in Society 12
Part 1: Crafting the Political Enemy: The Power of Propaganda in Politics 17
Chapter 1: The Foundation of Enemy Creation: Analyzing Opponents and Public Perception 20
Chapter 2: Turning Opponents into Villains: The Art of Political Demonization 26
Chapter 3: Harnessing the Media: Spreading Fear and Shaping Perception 34
Chapter 4: Constructing the Threat: Amplifying Fear to Unite the Masses 42
Part 2: Enemies of Faith: How Religion Constructs and Sustains the Idea of Opposition 51
Chapter 5: Constructing the Enemy of Faith: Framing Ideological Opposition as a Threat 53
Chapter 6: Binding Through Fear: Techniques for Uniting Followers in Faith 60
Chapter 7: The Modern Adversary: Exploiting Cultural Shifts and Amplifying Threats 68
Chapter 8: Crafting the Enemy: A Practical Guide for Religious Leaders 78
Part 3: Dividing to Conquer: Social Division and the Power of Group Dynamics 89

Chapter 9: The Power of Division: Creating Group Identity Through "Us vs. Them" 91
Chapter 10: Harnessing Opposition: Leveraging Social Movements for Identity and Mobilization 99
Chapter 11: Digital Echoes: The Role of Social Media in Propaganda and Division 114
Chapter 12: Strategies for Sustaining Unity: A Practical Guide for Group Leaders 125
Part 4: Nationalism and the Art of Enemy Creation 135
Chapter 13: Enemies Across Borders: Creating Foreign Threats Through Nationalism 138
Chapter 14: Rallying Through Symbols: The Power of National Symbols and Stories 144
Chapter 15: Modern Manipulation: Nationalist Propaganda in Today's World 154
Chapter 16: The Strategic Playbook: Using Nationalism to Build Foreign Threats 164
Part 5: The Mechanics of Manipulation: Practical Propaganda Techniques 173
Chapter 17: The Foundation of Influence: Crafting Effective Messaging 176
Chapter 18: Weaponizing Uncertainty: Using Fear and Misinformation 182
Chapter 19: Digital Domination: Leveraging Digital Platforms for Propaganda 192
Chapter 20: Silencing Dissent: Countering Opposition and Reinforcing Control 202
Part 6: The Price of Manipulation: Consequences and Ethical Considerations 212
Chapter 21: The Ripple Effects: Consequences of Creating Enemies 216
Chapter 22: Moral Boundaries: The Ethics of Propaganda 230

The Final Reflection: Power, Impact, and Responsibility of Propaganda.. 243
   Appendix: Tools for Understanding and Creating Influence 255

Creating the Enemy: Propaganda, Politics, and Public Perception

A.A. Castor

Dedication

To my beloved family,
Your unconditional love, unwavering support, and endless encouragement have been my greatest blessings. From the earliest days of dreaming to the challenging moments of writing, you have stood by me with patience and belief. This book is as much yours as it is mine, a reflection of the values you've instilled and the faith you've shown in me. Thank you for being my rock and my inspiration.

To my dear friends,
Your friendship has illuminated my path with laughter, shared moments, and invaluable support. You've cheered me on through every triumph and lifted me up through every challenge. Your belief in my endeavors has been a source of strength and motivation. This book is a testament to the power of friendship, and I am grateful for each of you who has walked this journey by my side.

To God,
Your grace and guidance have been my constant companions. In moments of doubt, you've shown me the way; in moments of joy, you've multiplied my gratitude. This book is a testament to your faithfulness and the blessings you've bestowed upon me. May it serve as a reflection of your love and the lessons you continue to teach me.

With heartfelt gratitude and love,
A.A. Castor

Copyright © 2024 by A.A. Castor

All rights reserved. No part of this book may be reproduced, stored in a retrieval system, or transmitted in any form or by any means—electronic, mechanical, photocopy, recording, scanning, or otherwise—except as permitted under Section 107 or 108 of the 1976 United States Copyright Act, without the prior written permission of the publisher, except for brief quotations embodied in critical reviews and certain other noncommercial uses permitted by copyright law.

For permission requests, contact A.A. Castor at:

Address: Urban Deca Home Metro Manila, 1230

Email: dev.castortony@gmail.com

Website: www.tonyc.info[1]

This book is a work of non-fiction. Names, characters, places, and incidents are either the product of the author's research or are used factually. Any resemblance to actual persons, living or dead, events, or locales is entirely coincidental.

Printed in Philippines

Philippine Copyright Law:

The Intellectual Property Code of the Philippines (Republic Act No. 8293) provides protection to literary and artistic works from the moment of their creation. It includes provisions for the rights of authors and copyright owners, including the exclusive right to reproduce, distribute, perform, and display their works. Unauthorized use or reproduction of copyrighted materials is subject to legal penalties under this law.

---

1. http://www.tonyc.info

Why I Am Writing This Book

The idea of propaganda is often viewed with suspicion—a tool for manipulation, deception, and control. Yet, it is an undeniable part of human history and society, used by leaders, governments, religious authorities, and even social movements to influence people and shape the course of events. As I researched and observed how propaganda has been utilized across cultures and timelines, I became fascinated not only by its effectiveness but also by its consequences. This book is born from a desire to explore the profound impact of propaganda, particularly the creation of enemies, and to shed light on the methods, effects, and moral considerations that come with wielding such power.

I am writing this book because I believe it is crucial to understand how narratives are crafted to shape public perception, instill fear, and unify people against a common enemy. Whether it's a politician rallying support by creating a scapegoat, a religious leader framing an ideology as a threat, or a country justifying conflict through nationalist rhetoric—propaganda is a powerful weapon that has shaped societies, both for better and for worse. By understanding these mechanisms, we can better recognize when we are being influenced, challenge the narratives presented to us, and make more informed decisions.

Another motivation for writing this book is to explore the ethical implications of using propaganda. As we see throughout history, the creation of enemies often leads to social division, discrimination, and conflict. The people who wield this tool hold immense power over the minds and actions of others, and with that power comes a great responsibility. It is easy to see the appeal of propaganda—its ability to rally people, to foster unity, and to achieve political objectives—but the cost is often far greater than the benefit. I want readers to think critically about the ethics involved and to consider whether the ends truly justify the means.

Moreover, I want to demystify propaganda for those who might think it is something used only by authoritarian regimes or in far-off conflicts. The reality is that propaganda is all around us—in political campaigns, advertising, media, and even in social media interactions. It is woven into the fabric of everyday life, often so subtly that we don't even notice its influence. By breaking down the techniques used and the psychology behind them, I hope to provide readers with the tools to identify and critically evaluate the propaganda they encounter, whether it's in the news, on social media, or from the leaders they look up to.

Finally, this book is a reflection on the responsibility that comes with the power to influence. Propaganda can be used to create positive change, to inspire people to come together for a common cause, and to foster hope in times of crisis. However, it can also be used to divide, to instill hatred, and to justify terrible actions. Those who wield this power must do so with caution, understanding the consequences of their actions and recognizing the impact they have on society and individuals. My aim is to provide a comprehensive exploration of both sides of propaganda—the power it holds and the responsibility it demands.

In writing this book, my hope is to empower readers to think critically, understand the true power of propaganda, and recognize the profound impact that it has on society, leadership, and individual lives. Whether you are a student, a leader, a communicator, or simply someone who wants to better understand the world around you, I invite you to explore this journey into the art, science, and ethics of creating enemies and shaping narratives.

Warning and Disclaimer

This book contains an in-depth exploration of the strategies, techniques, and historical examples of propaganda, including the deliberate creation of enemies and the manipulation of public perception. The purpose of this book is to educate readers about the mechanisms behind propaganda, the consequences of its use, and the ethical considerations involved. It is important to note that the content herein is intended for educational and analytical purposes only and should not be construed as an endorsement or encouragement of unethical behavior or harmful propaganda practices.

The techniques and strategies discussed in this book have been employed throughout history by various groups, institutions, and leaders, often with significant consequences. While understanding these methods is crucial for recognizing and resisting manipulation, they also possess the potential to cause harm if used irresponsibly. Readers are advised to approach the content with a critical mindset and to reflect on the moral and ethical implications of utilizing such techniques in any context.

The examples provided in this book are drawn from historical and contemporary case studies to illustrate the real-world applications and effects of propaganda. They are included for the purpose of analysis and discussion, not to glorify or justify the actions of those who used these methods. The goal is to offer readers a deeper understanding of how propaganda works, the power it holds, and the potential dangers it poses when used without regard for truth, ethics, and the well-being of society.

The author does not condone the use of propaganda to incite hatred, create enemies, or manipulate others for personal or political gain. The information presented is meant to foster critical thinking and awareness, enabling readers to recognize propaganda in their daily lives, understand its impact, and make informed decisions. It is the responsibility of each individual to use this knowledge ethically and to promote values of honesty, empathy, and respect for others.

By reading this book, you acknowledge that the content is provided for educational purposes only, and you agree to use the information responsibly. The author and publisher disclaim any liability for the misuse of the information contained herein and urge readers to consider the ethical consequences of their actions when applying the concepts discussed in this book.

About the Author

A.A. Castor is a dedicated writer and researcher with a deep passion for exploring the intersection of history, leadership, and strategy. His work spans a wide range of topics, including political strategy, social dynamics, philosophy, and governance. Castor's writing aims to uncover timeless lessons from the past, applying them to contemporary challenges to offer practical insights for personal and professional development.

Drawing inspiration from historical figures and pivotal moments, A.A. Castor examines the power structures, ideological battles, and social forces that shape the human experience. His work often delves into the use of propaganda, the dynamics of creating enemies, and the ethical dilemmas inherent in wielding influence over others. Castor blends historical analysis with leadership theory, engaging readers with compelling narratives that offer both historical context and actionable lessons for modern times.

In addition to his work as an author, A.A. Castor is an avid podcaster, sharing his thoughts on leadership, history, and social philosophy. He enjoys challenging conventional wisdom, encouraging his audience to question established norms and think critically about the forces that shape society. Through his writing and podcasting, Castor strives to inspire a deeper understanding of how power is used and the responsibilities that come with it.

A.A. Castor's research and writing are guided by a commitment to uncovering the truths of the past, the complexities of human behavior, and the ethical considerations of leadership. He invites readers to join him on a journey of exploration—one that challenges, informs, and ultimately empowers them to navigate the world with a greater awareness of the forces at play and the role they themselves can play in shaping a better future.

Introduction: Understanding the Role of Enemies in Society

Throughout history, leaders have recognized a fundamental truth about human nature: nothing unites people more effectively than a common enemy. Whether it is a political rival, a competing ideology, or an external threat, the concept of the enemy has served as a powerful tool for control and mobilization. In a world filled with complexity and nuance, an enemy offers simplicity—a clear target to blame for the hardships, fears, and insecurities faced by society. It is this clarity that makes the idea of an enemy not only compelling but necessary in maintaining power and fostering group cohesion.

Enemies serve multiple roles in the broader scheme of governance and influence. They become scapegoats for failures, rallying points during times of crisis, and symbols that can channel collective frustrations away from the establishment and onto an outsider. By designating a common adversary, leaders can forge unity among disparate and otherwise divided individuals. The notion of a shared struggle against a common foe enables a sense of belonging and purpose, transforming individual grievances into a unified cause.

This phenomenon is not limited to political systems; it extends to social movements, religious groups, and even nations. When leaders present a defined threat, it becomes easier for people to understand their place in the struggle and, by extension, their role within the group. Fear, once diffused and unfocused, now has a target. This focus allows leaders to harness fear and redirect it toward their enemies, transforming it into loyalty and commitment. People are drawn to certainty, and an enemy provides that certainty by simplifying complex social and political issues into an "us versus them" narrative.

One of the most notable examples of the power of an enemy is during times of war. Nations have long used the threat of an external adversary to foster a sense of national unity. In these moments, propaganda is deployed to dehumanize the enemy, turning them into faceless villains that must be defeated at all costs. This sense of urgency and moral righteousness allows citizens to feel part of something larger than themselves, to contribute to a fight that is framed as just and necessary. From the trenches of World War I to the ideological battlegrounds of the Cold War, the construction of an enemy has been an essential part of rallying a nation's people behind a common goal.

But it is not only in war that the idea of an enemy plays a crucial role. Even in times of peace, leaders can manipulate the perception of internal threats to maintain control. By identifying an "enemy within"—be it political dissidents, minority groups, or any other segment that can be framed as a threat to the established order—leaders are able to create an atmosphere of fear and suspicion. This atmosphere allows those in power to justify extraordinary measures, such as curtailing civil liberties, increasing surveillance, or even launching campaigns of persecution. The perceived threat becomes a justification for actions that, under normal circumstances, would be deemed unacceptable.

Enemies are also a powerful tool in the hands of religious leaders. Throughout history, religions have framed their beliefs against those of "others," creating clear distinctions between believers and non-believers. The concept of the enemy of faith—a person, group, or idea that threatens the core beliefs of the community—has been used to rally the faithful and maintain doctrinal purity. The creation of such enemies serves to reinforce the authority of religious leaders, ensuring that their followers remain united against a perceived external or internal threat. By painting certain ideologies, behaviors, or even other religions as dangerous, leaders can strengthen the collective identity of their group and keep dissent in check.

The enemy narrative is not limited to national or religious leaders; it can also be observed in social movements and group dynamics. Activists, in seeking to highlight injustices and mobilize support, often identify a clear adversary—an establishment, institution, or ideology that embodies the issues they oppose. This approach allows for the simplification of complex social issues into a binary conflict, making it easier for individuals to identify and engage with the movement. The "enemy" becomes the focal point for grievances, providing a clear and compelling reason for action. This tactic can be highly effective in generating momentum and drawing attention to a cause, but it also risks creating deep social divisions.

In the modern era, with the advent of mass communication and social media, the creation of enemies has become even more pervasive. Information—and misinformation—can be disseminated instantly to millions of people, and narratives can be amplified or distorted at an unprecedented scale. Leaders can use these tools to shape public perception, leveraging algorithms that reinforce existing biases and create echo chambers where enemy narratives are continuously validated. The rapid spread of propaganda allows leaders to keep the public in a constant state of agitation, ensuring that the enemy remains a clear and present danger in the minds of their followers.

The power of propaganda lies in its ability to shape perceptions, often molding ordinary individuals into fierce defenders of a cause. By repeating specific narratives and using emotional triggers, leaders cultivate a reality where enemies are not merely adversaries—they are the embodiment of evil, standing in stark opposition to the values and identity of the group. This process dehumanizes the enemy, making them a symbol of everything that must be opposed, and thus justifying any actions taken against them. When an enemy is stripped of their humanity, empathy fades, and the door is opened to acts of violence and repression that would otherwise be unthinkable.

However, while the role of enemies is indeed powerful, it also demands careful consideration. The deliberate choice to create an enemy is not without ethical implications. Propaganda campaigns designed to construct enemies can lead to violence, discrimination, and lasting societal divisions. The demonization of others often results in the erosion of empathy, the collapse of rational discourse, and the perpetuation of hatred. History is replete with examples where the relentless pursuit of an "enemy" has resulted in atrocities and suffering—realities that continue to shape our world today. From the witch hunts of medieval Europe to the ethnic cleansings of the 20th century, the consequences of enemy-making can be devastating.

The decision to create an adversary is a calculated move that can yield both remarkable unity and devastating consequences. This balance between control and chaos underscores the complexity of propaganda and enemy creation, raising important questions about the responsibilities of leadership and the ethical boundaries that must be navigated. Leaders who wish to consolidate power, influence masses, or unify their followers must grapple with the potent force of enemy-making, understanding that while it may serve their immediate goals, the long-term consequences can be profound and often uncontrollable.

Creating an enemy is an act that wields incredible power—a power that has shaped empires, toppled governments, and forged movements that changed the course of history. The calculated construction of an adversary is more than just a political maneuver; it is a strategic decision that determines how people perceive the world, themselves, and others. The purpose of this book is to illuminate the mechanisms behind this phenomenon, exploring the methods and strategies that leaders use to turn opponents into enemies while offering practical insights into wielding this powerful tool. By understanding the dynamics of enemy creation, readers can learn not only how to use propaganda effectively but also the broader implications of wielding such influence over the minds and hearts of people.

Part 1: Crafting the Political Enemy: The Power of Propaganda in Politics

In the world of politics, perception often matters more than reality. The ability to control narratives, shape public opinion, and cast opponents in a negative light can mean the difference between victory and defeat. Political propaganda is not merely about promoting one's own image; it is just as much about tarnishing the image of the opponent, creating an "enemy" that the public will rally against. This practice has been a cornerstone of political strategy for centuries, from the sophisticated rhetoric of ancient empires to the media-driven campaigns of the modern age.

The process of crafting a political enemy is both art and science. It involves a careful study of the opponent's weaknesses and an understanding of the fears and desires of the public. Successful propaganda taps into existing sentiments, amplifying doubts and fears while positioning the opponent as a threat to the well-being of the people. Through strategic framing, a political rival can be transformed from a mere competitor into a villain whose actions and intentions are portrayed as fundamentally harmful. It is a transformation that requires precision, timing, and an acute awareness of public perception.

The first step in this process is understanding the opponent—identifying vulnerabilities, inconsistencies, and flaws that can be exploited. By understanding what the opponent represents and where their weaknesses lie, it becomes possible to construct a narrative that casts them as a danger to the values and stability of society. Propaganda is not simply about exaggerating flaws; it is about constructing a story that resonates with the public. It is about turning the opponent into an embodiment of everything that is wrong, creating a scapegoat for the public's fears and frustrations.

The art of demonizing opponents goes beyond mere criticism. It involves painting them as fundamentally untrustworthy or dangerous, using a combination of rhetorical strategies, emotive language, and visual symbolism. It requires the use of fear—often irrational—to shape perceptions and create an emotional reaction that overrides logical thinking. This emotional manipulation can make even a minor flaw seem catastrophic, transforming a benign policy disagreement into a perceived existential threat. Political propaganda uses language that evokes strong emotions—anger, fear, and disgust—driving people to oppose the enemy with fervor.

Media manipulation plays a critical role in this process. By controlling the flow of information and emphasizing certain stories while downplaying or ignoring others, leaders can craft a narrative that supports their portrayal of the enemy. The media becomes a tool for spreading fear, exaggerating threats, and repeating key messages until they become ingrained in the public's consciousness. The use of soundbites, catchy slogans, and powerful visuals can make complex issues seem simple, driving home the idea that the enemy must be opposed at all costs. The media serves not only to inform but also to persuade, redirecting the audience's attention in ways that serve the propagandist's goals.

Building a narrative of threat is crucial to solidifying the enemy's status. Through the language of fear, leaders can amplify the perceived danger posed by their opponents, creating a sense of urgency that demands immediate action. This sense of urgency prevents rational deliberation and pushes people toward a fight-or-flight response, causing them to align with the propagandist for protection. It is not enough to identify an opponent as flawed; they must be seen as a direct and immediate threat to the values, safety, and identity of the people.

By constructing a narrative that frames the opponent as dangerous, the propagandist transforms public sentiment, redirecting anxieties and frustrations toward a common enemy.

This part of the book will explore the intricacies of political propaganda, diving deep into the strategies and techniques that have been used throughout history to create and sustain political enemies. It will provide practical guidance on how to identify weaknesses, manipulate media, and craft fear-driven narratives to effectively turn a political opponent into an enemy. Through historical examples and practical insights, the chapters ahead will reveal the powerful role propaganda plays in shaping political landscapes and controlling public perception.

Chapter 1: The Foundation of Enemy Creation: Analyzing Opponents and Public Perception

Every successful propaganda campaign begins with a thorough understanding of the opponent. Before crafting a narrative that paints a political figure as the enemy, it is crucial to identify and exploit their vulnerabilities. Political opponents, like anyone else, have weaknesses—whether in their policy positions, their personal history, or their connections. These weaknesses can serve as the foundation for building a compelling enemy narrative that resonates with the public. By exposing and amplifying these vulnerabilities, the opponent can be turned into a symbol of failure, incompetence, or even moral corruption.

Identifying weaknesses requires careful research and analysis. It involves examining the opponent's track record, statements, and associations to uncover inconsistencies, mistakes, and elements that could be viewed negatively. Weaknesses may be hidden in policy contradictions, past decisions, or personal missteps. The goal is to gather enough material that can be woven into a cohesive and persuasive story—one that casts doubt on the opponent's capability and character. This process requires attention to detail and a strategic approach, ensuring that the chosen weaknesses align with the narrative that is being constructed.

However, identifying weaknesses alone is not enough. It is equally important to assess public sentiment to understand what issues and narratives will resonate most effectively with the audience. Public perception is shaped by cultural values, current events, and collective emotions. By gauging what the public fears, desires, and values, the propagandist can tailor their messaging to align with these sentiments, ensuring that the enemy narrative strikes a chord with the people. Assessing public sentiment involves understanding the concerns that are most pressing to the community, the values they hold dear, and the anxieties that keep them up at night.

The art of propaganda lies in making the audience feel that the opponent's weaknesses are directly connected to their own fears and problems. If the public is worried about economic instability, for instance, the opponent must be framed as a threat to economic security. If there is a fear of cultural change, the opponent must be portrayed as someone who jeopardizes traditional values. The key is to create a link between the weaknesses of the opponent and the perceived dangers facing the public. This connection makes the enemy narrative feel personal, ensuring that people will not only believe it but also feel compelled to act against the opponent.

Understanding the opponent and public sentiment forms the basis of any effective propaganda campaign. It is the groundwork upon which the narrative is built, ensuring that the portrayal of the enemy is not only compelling but also relevant to the audience. By accurately assessing both the opponent's vulnerabilities and the public's concerns, the propagandist can craft a message that resonates deeply, laying the foundation for turning a political rival into a feared and despised enemy.

Exploiting Vulnerabilities: Identifying the Weaknesses of Your Opponent

TO CREATE A COMPELLING enemy narrative, the first step is to thoroughly understand the opponent—specifically, to identify and exploit their weaknesses. The effectiveness of any propaganda campaign hinges on its ability to make the opponent appear flawed, dangerous, or incompetent. The process of identifying weaknesses is not merely about uncovering facts; it is about understanding what aspects of the opponent's character, behavior, or policies can be turned into liabilities in the eyes of the public.

The weaknesses of an opponent can come from various sources. They may be rooted in their personal history, including past controversies, scandals, or relationships that could be viewed negatively. Mistakes from their political career, such as unpopular decisions or policies that failed, provide ample ammunition for creating a negative image. These past actions can be reframed to paint the opponent as either incompetent or having malicious intentions. By emphasizing and exaggerating these flaws, the propagandist can create an indelible association between the opponent and failure.

Another effective strategy is to look for inconsistencies between what the opponent says and what they do. Hypocrisy is a powerful tool for discrediting an opponent, as it creates an image of untrustworthiness. When an opponent's words and actions contradict each other, it becomes easy to frame them as dishonest and self-serving. Highlighting these inconsistencies repeatedly can erode public trust, making it difficult for the opponent to gain credibility. The goal is to create doubt, to ensure that whenever the opponent speaks, the audience questions their sincerity and intentions.

Analyzing the opponent's current position and policy stances is another avenue for identifying weaknesses. Every policy comes with drawbacks, and even well-intentioned proposals can have unintended consequences. By focusing on these potential downsides, and presenting them in a way that emphasizes the risks, the propagandist can create a sense of danger around the opponent's ideas. This not only undermines the opponent's credibility but also shifts the narrative to make them appear as a direct threat to the public's safety and well-being. The aim is to make the opponent's policies appear not just flawed, but potentially disastrous.

In addition to identifying the weaknesses inherent in the opponent's actions and character, it is essential to understand the cultural and social context in which the propaganda will be received. This involves assessing what the public values, fears, and despises. Once these elements are clear, the opponent's weaknesses can be framed in a way that resonates most effectively with the audience. For instance, if the public values stability, portraying the opponent as reckless and unpredictable will create a powerful negative association. If there are prevailing fears—such as economic decline or cultural change—linking the opponent to these fears will amplify the impact of the propaganda.

Identifying the weaknesses of an opponent is not just about uncovering flaws but about framing those flaws in a way that aligns with public sentiment. By combining an understanding of the opponent's vulnerabilities with insights into what concerns the public, the propagandist can craft a narrative that is both compelling and emotionally resonant. The result is an enemy that is not just disliked, but actively feared and opposed, laying the foundation for an effective propaganda campaign.

Understanding the Pulse: Assessing Public Sentiment

ASSESSING PUBLIC SENTIMENT is a crucial component of any successful propaganda campaign. To effectively craft an enemy narrative, it is not enough to simply identify the weaknesses of the opponent—those weaknesses must also align with the fears, values, and concerns of the public. Understanding what motivates and worries the audience allows the propagandist to create a message that resonates deeply, making the enemy narrative not only believable but emotionally impactful.

Public sentiment is shaped by a complex mix of factors, including cultural values, economic conditions, historical experiences, and current events. A successful propagandist must stay attuned to the mood of the population, understanding what issues are most pressing and which emotions can be harnessed to their advantage. This means being aware of the prevailing fears—whether they are related to safety, economic security, or cultural identity—and using those fears to frame the opponent as the primary threat to what the public holds dear.

One of the key methods for assessing public sentiment is through media analysis. News outlets, social media platforms, and public forums offer valuable insights into what people are thinking and feeling at any given time. Monitoring these channels allows the propagandist to identify trending topics, popular opinions, and emerging concerns. For example, if economic uncertainty is a major topic in the news, the opponent can be framed as someone who will exacerbate these economic woes, making them appear as a direct threat to the financial stability of the average citizen.

Social media, in particular, is an invaluable tool for gauging public sentiment. It provides real-time feedback on what people are talking about, what they are worried about, and how they are reacting to events. By analyzing posts, comments, and shares, the propagandist can identify which messages resonate with the audience and adjust their strategy accordingly. Social media also allows for direct interaction with the public, enabling the propagandist to test different narratives and see which ones generate the strongest emotional responses. This constant feedback loop ensures that the propaganda remains relevant and effective.

Polling and surveys are also powerful tools for assessing public sentiment. Conducting surveys that gauge people's attitudes towards specific issues, policies, or public figures provides concrete data that can guide the development of the enemy narrative. The results of these surveys can reveal what concerns the public most—whether it is crime, unemployment, corruption, or a perceived decline in moral values. Armed with this knowledge, the propagandist can craft a message that directly addresses these concerns, positioning the opponent as the embodiment of everything the public fears or dislikes.

In addition to understanding fears and concerns, it is important to identify what the public values and aspires to. Propaganda is most effective when it not only plays on fears but also appeals to positive emotions, such as patriotism, family values, or the desire for stability. By framing the opponent as someone who threatens these cherished values, the propagandist can create a powerful emotional reaction that drives people to oppose the enemy with passion and conviction. The key is to create a connection between the opponent's perceived weaknesses and the values that the public holds dear, ensuring that the enemy narrative feels personal and immediate.

Assessing public sentiment is an ongoing process. As events unfold and the mood of the population shifts, the propagandist must be ready to adapt their message to maintain its relevance. A narrative that resonated yesterday may no longer be effective if the public's attention has shifted to a new issue. Therefore, constant monitoring and flexibility are essential to ensure that the enemy narrative continues to align with the public's concerns and emotions. By staying attuned to the pulse of the population, the propagandist can craft a narrative that not only resonates but also compels the audience to action, turning the opponent into a feared and despised enemy.

Chapter 2: Turning Opponents into Villains: The Art of Political Demonization

Once the weaknesses of a political opponent have been identified, the next step is to transform them from a mere rival into a full-fledged villain in the eyes of the public. Demonizing an opponent is an art that requires a nuanced understanding of language, psychology, and the power of framing. It involves taking ordinary flaws or mistakes and magnifying them to the point where they become symbols of something fundamentally threatening. Through careful use of rhetoric, strategic framing, and repetition, an opponent can be portrayed as not just flawed, but dangerous—a figure who must be opposed for the sake of society's well-being.

The key to successful demonization lies in rhetorical strategies and framing. Language has the power to evoke emotions, and the right choice of words can turn an opponent from a mere critic into an existential threat. Negative labeling, derogatory terms, and emotive language can create a powerful image of the opponent as corrupt, untrustworthy, or malicious. By framing their actions and intentions in the worst possible light, their character can be systematically dismantled. Even ordinary actions, when framed effectively, can be made to appear sinister—suggesting ulterior motives or painting them as a threat to the public's safety and values.

Framing is equally important in creating a villain. It involves deciding how to present information in a way that aligns with the desired narrative. By selectively emphasizing certain aspects of the opponent's actions while ignoring others, the propagandist can create a distorted yet compelling image. For example, highlighting an opponent's association with a controversial figure or portraying their policy proposals as reckless and harmful can influence how the public perceives them. The frame within which the information is presented determines whether the audience views the opponent as a well-intentioned leader or a villain whose actions are detrimental to society.

Historical examples of political demonization provide powerful lessons in how effective this technique can be. From the character assassinations carried out during the height of political revolutions to the demonization campaigns of the 20th century that justified authoritarian rule, history is filled with instances where opponents have been successfully turned into villains. Leaders have used these strategies to not only discredit their rivals but also to rally their own supporters, creating a sense of urgency and moral clarity that drives collective action.

In this chapter, the focus will be on understanding the tools and techniques that make demonization so effective. The use of rhetorical devices such as hyperbole, insinuation, and fear-mongering will be explored, along with practical examples of how framing has been used to sway public opinion. By studying historical examples, it becomes evident how the art of demonizing opponents has shaped political landscapes, creating villains that unified the masses under a common cause. The goal of this chapter is to equip the reader with the knowledge and techniques needed to effectively turn a political opponent into an enemy—a figure who must be opposed for the good of the people.

Crafting the Villain: Rhetorical Strategies and Framing Techniques

CREATING A VILLAIN out of a political opponent involves more than simply pointing out flaws—it requires a strategic use of language and narrative framing to turn those flaws into something sinister. The goal is to craft a story that makes the opponent appear not just wrong, but dangerous, morally corrupt, or fundamentally opposed to the well-being of the public. This transformation relies on a combination of rhetorical strategies and framing techniques that evoke emotional responses and shape perception in a way that aligns with the propagandist's objectives.

Rhetorical strategies are essential for creating a compelling villain. One of the most effective techniques is the use of emotive language—words that evoke strong feelings such as fear, anger, or disgust. By choosing language that triggers emotional reactions, the propagandist can make the opponent seem threatening and untrustworthy. For example, instead of describing an opponent's actions as "mistakes," they might be framed as "reckless decisions" or "dangerous policies." The choice of words matters, as it determines whether the audience perceives the opponent's actions as minor errors or as catastrophic threats to society.

Hyperbole is another powerful rhetorical tool for villain creation. By exaggerating the opponent's flaws or the consequences of their actions, the propagandist can amplify fear and urgency. A minor policy disagreement can be framed as an existential threat, with phrases like "this will destroy our way of life" or "this is the beginning of the end for our values." The purpose of hyperbole is to make the stakes appear so high that the audience feels compelled to act, believing that the opponent's influence must be countered at all costs.

Another effective strategy is the use of insinuation and implication. Rather than making direct accusations, insinuations allow the propagandist to plant doubts in the minds of the audience without needing concrete evidence. For example, suggesting that the opponent "might have connections to corrupt figures" or that they are "rumored to have a hidden agenda" creates a sense of suspicion. These insinuations are often more effective than direct accusations because they encourage the audience to draw their own conclusions, making the resulting mistrust feel more personal and less imposed.

Framing techniques work hand-in-hand with rhetorical strategies to create a cohesive and persuasive narrative. Framing involves presenting information in a way that emphasizes certain aspects while downplaying or ignoring others. It is about controlling the lens through which the audience views the opponent, ensuring that only the negative aspects are highlighted. For instance, an opponent's policy that has both positive and negative aspects can be framed exclusively in terms of its potential harm, thereby shaping the audience's perception in a negative direction.

One framing technique is the use of selective storytelling. This involves choosing specific incidents or examples that support the desired narrative while ignoring any contradictory evidence. For example, if the opponent has made several successful policy decisions, but one policy led to unintended negative consequences, the propagandist will focus exclusively on the negative outcome. By repeating this story and ignoring the successes, the opponent is framed as incompetent or harmful, regardless of their overall track record.

Another powerful framing technique is association. By associating the opponent with negative symbols, ideas, or individuals, the propagandist can transfer the negative perception onto the opponent. This could involve linking the opponent to unpopular figures, controversial ideologies, or historical failures. For instance, suggesting that the opponent's policies are reminiscent of a past leader who is widely disliked creates an immediate negative connection in the audience's mind. Association works on a psychological level, making it difficult for the audience to separate the opponent from the negative imagery they are linked to.

Repetition is a fundamental element in both rhetorical strategies and framing. A message, no matter how exaggerated or baseless, becomes more believable when it is repeated often enough. By consistently repeating key phrases, negative labels, and framed narratives, the propagandist ensures that these ideas become ingrained in the audience's perception. Over time, the repeated narrative becomes accepted as common knowledge, and the opponent's image as a villain solidifies in the minds of the public.

Crafting a villain is about controlling the narrative, ensuring that every aspect of the opponent's public image is framed in a way that aligns with the propagandist's goals. By using emotive language, hyperbole, insinuation, and selective storytelling, the propagandist creates a powerful emotional reaction in the audience. Through association, framing, and repetition, the negative image of the opponent becomes fixed, turning them into a villain who embodies all that must be opposed. These techniques are the building blocks of effective propaganda, transforming a political rival into a threat that unites and mobilizes the masses against a common enemy.

Lessons from History: Effective Political Demonization in Action

THROUGHOUT HISTORY, political demonization has been used as a powerful tool to turn rivals into enemies, manipulating public perception and consolidating power. Examining historical examples provides valuable insights into how propaganda has been employed effectively to create villains out of political opponents. These cases illustrate the power of rhetoric, framing, and media manipulation in shaping public opinion and ensuring that an enemy narrative takes hold in the collective consciousness.

One of the most famous examples of effective political demonization is the portrayal of Maximilien Robespierre during the French Revolution. Robespierre, a leading figure in the Reign of Terror, was initially seen as a champion of the people. However, when political tides began to turn, his opponents used propaganda to cast him as a tyrant and a threat to the revolution itself. They amplified his role in the mass executions, labeled him as a dictator, and spread fear about his growing power. The narrative of Robespierre as an authoritarian figure who betrayed the ideals of the revolution gained traction, ultimately leading to his downfall and execution. The effective use of fear and the emphasis on his supposed betrayal turned public sentiment against him, demonstrating the potency of framing a political leader as a villain.

Another notable example is the demonization of the Bolsheviks during the Russian Civil War. The White Army, made up of anti-Bolshevik forces, used propaganda extensively to paint the Bolsheviks as enemies of the Russian people and culture. The Bolsheviks were depicted as violent extremists who threatened traditional values and the fabric of Russian society. Posters, pamphlets, and speeches portrayed the Bolsheviks as godless radicals who sought to destroy religion, family, and social order. The emphasis on the supposed moral corruption of the Bolsheviks played into the fears of many Russians, particularly the rural population, and helped rally support for the White Army. Although the White Army ultimately failed, their propaganda campaign left a lasting legacy, with the Bolsheviks continuing to face suspicion and resistance even after their victory.

A more recent example of effective political demonization can be seen in the United States during the Cold War, particularly in the McCarthy era. Senator Joseph McCarthy and his allies used propaganda to demonize anyone they suspected of having communist sympathies. They labeled these individuals as un-American, dangerous, and a threat to national security. By equating communism with treason, McCarthy effectively created a climate of fear and paranoia, where anyone could be accused and have their reputation destroyed. The term "Red Scare" became synonymous with the fear of communism, and the demonization of supposed communist sympathizers led to widespread blacklisting, loss of employment, and even imprisonment. The use of fear-driven rhetoric and the association of communism with betrayal and danger allowed McCarthy to wield significant power, even without concrete evidence to support his claims.

In Nazi Germany, the demonization of Jews serves as one of the most extreme and tragic examples of political propaganda. The Nazi regime, under Adolf Hitler, systematically used propaganda to portray Jews as the root cause of Germany's economic woes and social problems. Through posters, films, speeches, and educational materials, Jews were depicted as parasitic, deceitful, and fundamentally opposed to the interests of the German people. The propaganda campaign dehumanized Jews, framing them as enemies who needed to be eradicated for the good of the nation. This systematic demonization laid the groundwork for public acceptance of the Holocaust, demonstrating the horrific power of propaganda when it is used to create an enemy narrative that justifies violence and persecution.

Another instance of political demonization occurred during the Rwandan Genocide in 1994. The Hutu-led government used state-controlled radio and newspapers to demonize the Tutsi minority. The Tutsis were labeled as "cockroaches" and portrayed as existential threats to the Hutu population. This dehumanizing language was repeated constantly, fostering hatred and fear among the Hutu majority. By framing the Tutsis as dangerous enemies who needed to be eliminated, the propagandists incited ordinary citizens to participate in acts of violence and mass murder. The effective use of simple, emotive language and repetition made the enemy narrative deeply ingrained, leading to one of the most devastating genocides in modern history.

These historical examples demonstrate that effective political demonization relies on a combination of rhetoric, repetition, and framing that connects the opponent to the fears and insecurities of the population. Whether through the use of dehumanizing language, the amplification of threats, or the association of opponents with dangerous ideologies, the goal is always the same: to create a powerful emotional reaction that overrides rational thinking and compels the audience to act against the perceived enemy. By studying these examples, it becomes clear how the techniques of demonization can be used to shape public perception, rally support, and eliminate opposition, often with devastating consequences.

Chapter 3: Harnessing the Media: Spreading Fear and Shaping Perception

In the battle for public opinion, media is the most powerful weapon at a propagandist's disposal. The ability to manipulate media channels allows leaders to reach vast audiences, crafting narratives that shape perception and influence behavior. Media manipulation is not just about disseminating information; it is about controlling the narrative, determining what people see, hear, and ultimately believe. By using media strategically, political actors can spread fear, sow distrust, and create a sense of urgency that compels the public to rally against a common enemy.

The use of fear is a particularly potent tool in media manipulation. Fear bypasses rational thought and triggers emotional responses, making it easier to influence behavior. By presenting selective information, exaggerating threats, and constantly reminding the audience of the dangers posed by the opponent, media can create a climate of anxiety and suspicion. This fear-driven narrative serves to frame the opponent as an imminent threat, someone who must be stopped for the safety and stability of society. The constant repetition of such messages through multiple media channels ensures that the fear takes root, eventually becoming a part of the collective consciousness.

Crafting effective soundbites and visuals is another crucial element of media manipulation. In a world where attention spans are short and information overload is the norm, it is essential to communicate complex ideas in a way that is easily digestible and emotionally impactful. Soundbites—short, memorable phrases—can be used to distill the enemy narrative into a few powerful words that resonate with the public. These soundbites are designed to evoke strong emotions, whether it is anger, fear, or indignation, and are repeated across media platforms to reinforce the intended message. Similarly, powerful visuals—images that evoke strong feelings or symbolize the threat posed by the opponent—can be used to leave a lasting impression on the audience.

The media also plays a crucial role in controlling the flow of information. By determining what stories get coverage and how they are framed, propagandists can shape the public's perception of events. Highlighting stories that align with the desired narrative while ignoring those that contradict it creates a biased but compelling version of reality. By carefully curating the information presented to the public, the propagandist ensures that the audience's view of the opponent is shaped entirely by the negative narrative being pushed.

This chapter will delve into the various techniques used to manipulate the media for political gains. It will explore how to use different media channels—television, radio, social media, and print—to spread fear and distrust effectively. Additionally, it will provide practical guidance on crafting impactful soundbites and visuals that stick in the public's mind and shape their perception of the opponent. By understanding and mastering the tools of media manipulation, a propagandist can ensure that their portrayal of the enemy is not only heard but also believed by the masses.

Amplifying Anxiety: Using Media Channels to Spread Fear and Distrust

MEDIA IS THE MOST POTENT tool in spreading propaganda, and using it effectively allows for the amplification of fear and the sowing of distrust in the minds of the public. When attempting to create an enemy, controlling the narrative is crucial, and media channels—whether traditional outlets like television and newspapers or modern platforms like social media—provide the necessary reach to influence and manipulate public perception. By leveraging these channels, propagandists can ensure that their messages of fear and distrust reach as many people as possible, creating an atmosphere where the enemy is seen as an imminent and pervasive threat.

Television and radio are powerful tools for reaching large audiences quickly and delivering emotionally charged messages. These platforms allow for the repeated broadcast of speeches, soundbites, and news segments that are designed to highlight the supposed dangers posed by the enemy. The goal is to make fear a constant presence in the daily lives of the audience. By frequently airing stories about the opponent's supposed misdeeds or the threats they pose, the propagandist can keep the audience in a state of heightened anxiety. The repetition of these messages helps solidify the enemy narrative, ensuring that it becomes an accepted truth in the minds of viewers and listeners.

The visual aspect of television also plays a critical role in spreading fear. Imagery has a powerful impact on human emotions, and using specific visuals to depict the enemy can evoke strong feelings of anger, fear, or disgust. For example, showing footage of protests, unrest, or violent incidents while linking them to the opponent helps create an association between the enemy and chaos. The use of dramatic visuals—such as images of destruction, angry crowds, or menacing symbols—can have a lasting effect on the audience, reinforcing the idea that the opponent is a dangerous and destabilizing force. The careful selection of images and video clips is crucial in building an emotional narrative that portrays the enemy as a direct threat to society.

Print media, such as newspapers and magazines, also serves as an important channel for spreading fear and distrust. Articles, editorials, and opinion pieces can be used to provide "evidence" of the enemy's intentions and to frame their actions in a negative light. By presenting biased or selective information as objective reporting, print media can lend credibility to the propagandist's narrative. Headlines are particularly effective in grabbing attention and creating an immediate emotional reaction. Sensationalist headlines that use charged language, such as "The Threat Within" or "A Danger to Our Values," set the tone for how the audience will perceive the content, even if they do not read the entire article. The printed word has an air of authority, and using it to spread distrust can have a significant impact on shaping public opinion.

Social media, however, is perhaps the most powerful tool for spreading fear and distrust in the modern era. Unlike traditional media, social media allows for rapid dissemination of information and enables direct interaction with the audience. Propagandists can use social media platforms to spread their messages widely, employing tactics such as sharing alarming stories, posting emotionally charged content, and creating viral hashtags that draw attention to the perceived threat. The interactive nature of social media also allows for the creation of echo chambers, where like-minded individuals reinforce each other's beliefs, amplifying fear and distrust without the interference of opposing viewpoints. This environment makes it easy for misinformation to spread, as people are more likely to accept and share content that aligns with their existing fears.

Another advantage of social media is the ability to use bots and fake accounts to create the illusion of widespread support for the enemy narrative. By flooding platforms with posts that echo the propagandist's messages, it becomes possible to create a sense of consensus, making the enemy narrative appear more credible and widely accepted. When people see that others are expressing the same fears and distrust, they are more likely to adopt those views themselves. This creates a self-perpetuating cycle of fear and distrust, as the audience becomes both consumers and disseminators of the propaganda.

Talk shows, podcasts, and interviews are also effective channels for spreading fear. These formats allow for more in-depth discussions that can explore the supposed dangers posed by the enemy in greater detail. The use of "experts" and analysts lends credibility to the fear-driven narrative, giving the impression that the threat is real and well-documented. By presenting selective data or anecdotal evidence, these discussions can make the case against the opponent seem rational and well-supported, even if the underlying information is flawed or manipulated. The conversational nature of these formats makes them more relatable, allowing the audience to feel as though they are receiving insider knowledge about a pressing threat.

Ultimately, the effective use of media channels to spread fear and distrust is about saturating the information environment with the enemy narrative. The goal is to ensure that the audience is constantly exposed to messages that reinforce the idea of the opponent as a threat, leaving little room for alternative viewpoints. By using television, radio, print, social media, and other platforms in a coordinated effort, the propagandist can create a pervasive sense of danger and distrust that mobilizes the public against the enemy. The more people see, hear, and read about the threat, the more deeply ingrained the fear becomes, ensuring that the enemy narrative takes hold and drives collective action.

Memorable Messages: Crafting Effective Soundbites and Visuals for Impact

IN A WORLD SATURATED with information, capturing and holding the public's attention is a significant challenge. To effectively demonize an opponent, it is crucial to distill complex ideas into simple, memorable messages that resonate with the audience. Soundbites and visuals are two of the most powerful tools for achieving this, as they have the ability to convey an entire narrative in a matter of seconds.

A well-crafted soundbite or an impactful visual can evoke strong emotions, create lasting impressions, and drive home the propagandist's message, ensuring that it sticks with the audience long after they have seen or heard it.

Soundbites are short, catchy phrases that distill the essence of a message into a form that is easy to remember and repeat. The effectiveness of a soundbite lies in its simplicity and emotional resonance. It should be direct, impactful, and evoke a strong emotional response, whether that response is fear, anger, or indignation. For example, referring to an opponent as a "threat to our freedom" or "an enemy of the people" instantly conveys a sense of danger and positions the opponent as someone who must be opposed. The language used in a soundbite should be evocative, using powerful words that leave no room for ambiguity. The goal is to make the message resonate so deeply that it becomes a part of the audience's understanding of the opponent.

Repetition is a key element in the effectiveness of soundbites. A phrase that is repeated often enough begins to feel true, even if there is little evidence to support it. By using the same soundbite across multiple media channels—television, radio, social media, and print—the propagandist ensures that the message is heard over and over again, embedding itself in the public consciousness. The repetition of soundbites creates a sense of familiarity, and the more familiar a message becomes, the more likely people are to believe it. This is why slogans and soundbites are so often used in political campaigns—they are easy to remember, easy to repeat, and they create an emotional connection with the audience.

Another important aspect of crafting effective soundbites is tailoring them to the specific fears, values, and concerns of the audience. For instance, if the audience is particularly concerned about economic stability, a soundbite like "Their policies will destroy our economy" will be more effective than a generic attack. The soundbite must tap into what the audience cares about most, making the threat feel personal and immediate. This personalization ensures that the message resonates on an emotional level, compelling the audience to view the opponent as a direct danger to their way of life.

Visuals are just as powerful as words when it comes to shaping perception and evoking emotions. Images can convey complex messages instantly and can leave a lasting impact that words alone often cannot achieve. In the context of political demonization, visuals are used to create a specific image of the opponent—one that evokes fear, distrust, or even disgust. For example, using images of the opponent with harsh lighting, distorted colors, or unflattering angles can make them appear sinister or untrustworthy. The use of symbolism, such as placing the opponent next to images of destruction or chaos, reinforces the idea that they are a threat.

Propagandists also use visuals to create associations between the opponent and negative concepts or events. For instance, showing the opponent in the context of social unrest, violence, or failure can create a powerful visual link between them and these negative outcomes. The audience may not consciously notice these associations, but they can have a profound effect on how the opponent is perceived. The goal is to create a visual narrative that aligns with the verbal message being delivered—one that frames the opponent as a villain whose actions have dire consequences.

Visuals can also be used to evoke empathy for the audience's own group, making the opponent appear even more threatening by contrast. For example, showing images of happy, peaceful families or prosperous communities and then contrasting them with visuals of chaos, with the opponent framed as the cause of that chaos, creates a stark juxtaposition. This technique reinforces the idea that the opponent is a danger to everything that the audience values and holds dear.

Like soundbites, repetition is also important when it comes to visuals. The more often an audience sees a particular image or type of image associated with the opponent, the stronger the association becomes. Whether it is an unflattering photograph, a particular symbol, or a repeated visual motif, the constant exposure ensures that the image becomes part of the audience's mental picture of the opponent. Over time, these repeated visuals help solidify the opponent's identity as a villain, reinforcing the enemy narrative being pushed.

Crafting effective soundbites and visuals is about creating messages that are simple, emotionally charged, and easy to remember. By distilling complex ideas into memorable phrases and impactful images, the propagandist ensures that the audience not only understands the message but also feels it deeply. The combination of evocative language, powerful imagery, and constant repetition makes the enemy narrative resonate on both a rational and emotional level, leaving a lasting impression that shapes public perception and drives collective action against the opponent.

Chapter 4: Constructing the Threat: Amplifying Fear to Unite the Masses

Once the weaknesses of an opponent have been identified, and the media channels for disseminating the message are in place, the next step is to build a compelling narrative of threat. The goal is to portray the opponent as a danger not just to political ideals, but to the safety, well-being, and values of the people. The construction of a threat narrative is about taking existing fears and amplifying them, creating a sense of urgency that demands immediate action. By framing the opponent as an imminent and serious danger, a leader can mobilize support, divert attention from their own shortcomings, and unite the masses against a common enemy.

The language of fear is a crucial tool in amplifying threats. Words have power, and when chosen carefully, they can evoke visceral emotional responses that override logical thinking. The use of terms like "danger," "threat," "catastrophe," and "crisis" can instill a sense of panic in the audience, convincing them that they are on the brink of disaster. This type of language shifts the narrative from one of political competition to one of survival, where the opponent is not just a rival but an existential threat that must be eliminated to ensure the safety of society. The more immediate and severe the threat seems, the easier it becomes to justify extreme measures against the perceived enemy.

In addition to language, the timing and repetition of the threat narrative play a vital role in creating urgency. Repeated warnings about the dangers posed by the opponent reinforce the sense of a growing crisis, while strategic timing—linking the opponent to recent incidents or crises—can make the threat seem more real and immediate. By consistently emphasizing the risks and connecting them to the opponent, the propagandist ensures that the public's fear remains focused and sustained.

Building a narrative of threat also involves creating a story that people can relate to—one that connects the actions and beliefs of the opponent with the fears and concerns of the population. This means identifying what the audience cares about most—be it their security, livelihood, culture, or values—and framing the opponent as the primary danger to those things. By crafting a narrative where the opponent's actions directly threaten what the public holds dear, the propagandist transforms the enemy into the embodiment of all that must be resisted. It is a story of good versus evil, safety versus danger, and the stakes must be made clear to everyone involved.

This chapter will explore the techniques involved in building a narrative of threat. It will discuss the use of fear-driven language and the importance of repetition and timing to create a sense of urgency. Furthermore, practical strategies for linking the opponent's actions to public fears will be provided, along with examples of how such narratives have been effectively used in history. By mastering the art of constructing a threat narrative, a leader can turn an opponent into a villainous enemy, compelling the masses to stand together against a common and imminent danger.

Words of Alarm: The Language of Fear and Amplifying Threats to Create Urgency

THE LANGUAGE OF FEAR is one of the most powerful tools in the propagandist's arsenal. It has the ability to bypass rational thinking, tapping directly into the audience's emotions and triggering instinctual responses like fight or flight. When crafting an enemy narrative, amplifying threats and creating a sense of urgency is essential. By using fear-driven language, the propagandist can convince the audience that the danger posed by the opponent is not only real but also immediate, demanding action without hesitation. This emotional manipulation ensures that the enemy is perceived as a clear and present threat that must be countered at all costs.

The effectiveness of the language of fear lies in its ability to evoke powerful emotional reactions—reactions that override logical analysis. By using emotive words like "danger," "crisis," "catastrophe," and "threat," the propagandist creates a sense of impending doom. This type of language places the audience in a heightened state of alertness, making them more susceptible to manipulation. For example, describing an opponent's policy as "reckless" or "disastrous" implies that its consequences will be dire, regardless of the actual facts. The goal is to provoke an emotional reaction that leads the audience to view the opponent as a source of chaos and instability.

Fear-driven language is particularly effective when it targets specific concerns or vulnerabilities that the audience already has. By identifying what the audience fears most—whether it is economic collapse, threats to their safety, or cultural erosion—the propagandist can craft messages that amplify these fears and link them directly to the opponent. For instance, if the audience is concerned about crime, the opponent can be framed as someone who is "soft on crime" or even as actively enabling criminals. The use of fear to link the opponent with a specific threat makes the enemy narrative feel personal, as though the opponent's actions will directly impact the audience's safety and well-being.

Amplifying threats also involves exaggerating the potential consequences of the opponent's actions. Hyperbole is a key element in this process, as it takes an ordinary issue and blows it out of proportion, making it seem catastrophic. By suggesting that the opponent's actions will lead to "the collapse of society" or "the end of our freedoms," the propagandist makes the stakes appear incredibly high. This exaggeration creates a sense of urgency, convincing the audience that there is no time for debate or analysis—action must be taken immediately to counter the threat. The goal is to create a narrative in which the opponent is not just wrong but a direct and imminent danger to everything the audience values.

Another technique used in the language of fear is the creation of vague but ominous threats. By using phrases like "dark times ahead" or "a growing danger," the propagandist creates a sense of unease without providing specific details. This vagueness is intentional, as it allows the audience to project their own fears onto the opponent, making the threat feel even more personal and encompassing. The lack of specific evidence also makes it difficult to refute the claim, as the threat is implied rather than explicitly stated. The resulting uncertainty and anxiety make the audience more likely to accept the propagandist's narrative without question.

The language of fear is also effective when combined with calls to action. By pairing descriptions of threats with directives like "we must act now" or "we cannot afford to wait," the propagandist channels the audience's fear into a specific course of action. This action is almost always framed as opposing the enemy, reinforcing the idea that the opponent is the root cause of the danger. The sense of urgency created by the language of fear pushes the audience toward immediate action, leaving little room for dissent or alternative perspectives.

Repetition is key in ensuring that the language of fear takes hold. By repeatedly emphasizing the dangers posed by the opponent and the dire consequences of their actions, the propagandist ensures that the message becomes ingrained in the audience's mind. Over time, the repeated warnings and threats create a narrative in which the opponent is seen as an ever-present danger, one that must be dealt with to ensure the survival of the community. The more often the audience hears these fear-driven messages, the more likely they are to accept them as truth and to respond with the urgency that the propagandist desires.

The use of metaphors and analogies also enhances the effectiveness of fear-driven language. Comparing the opponent to a "cancer" that must be cut out, or describing their influence as a "ticking time bomb," creates vivid imagery that reinforces the idea of an urgent and growing threat. These metaphors make the danger feel tangible, something that is actively spreading and will cause irreparable harm if not stopped. By using such vivid language, the propagandist can create mental images that linger in the audience's mind, making the perceived threat even more visceral.

Words of alarm are carefully chosen to evoke fear, amplify perceived threats, and create a sense of urgency that compels action. By using emotive language, hyperbole, vagueness, repetition, and vivid metaphors, the propagandist ensures that the opponent is viewed as a direct and imminent danger to the audience's well-being. The language of fear is a powerful means of controlling perception, making the audience feel that they have no choice but to oppose the enemy for their own survival. In doing so, the propagandist transforms an ordinary political rival into a villain who must be defeated at all costs.

Crafting the Enemy: Practical Techniques for Creating an Enemy Narrative

CREATING AN EFFECTIVE enemy narrative is a strategic process that involves more than just pointing fingers or making accusations. It requires a careful construction of stories, symbols, and emotional cues that resonate with the audience, transforming an opponent into a figure who embodies everything that threatens the community. The enemy narrative must be persuasive, emotionally impactful, and, above all, repeated consistently until it becomes embedded in the collective mindset. Here are some practical techniques for creating such a narrative.

The first technique is **selective storytelling**. This involves choosing specific facts, incidents, or anecdotes that support the idea of the opponent as a threat while ignoring or downplaying anything that contradicts this image. Selective storytelling allows the propagandist to control the narrative by only presenting information that paints the enemy in the worst possible light. For example, if the opponent has a mixed record of both successes and failures, the focus will solely be on their failures, and even minor mistakes will be exaggerated to emphasize their incompetence or malevolence. The idea is to construct a consistent story that leaves the audience with a one-sided, negative impression of the opponent.

Labeling is another effective technique. Labels are simple yet powerful tools that create an instant association in the minds of the audience. Terms like "traitor," "extremist," "radical," or "corrupt" evoke strong emotions and frame the opponent in a specific, negative light. Once a label is attached to the opponent, it becomes difficult for them to shake off that perception. Repetition is key here—the more often the label is used, the more ingrained it becomes in public perception. The goal is to reduce the opponent to a single, negative identity, making it easier for the audience to accept them as the enemy.

Framing the opponent's intentions is crucial in creating an enemy narrative. It is not enough to criticize their actions; the propagandist must also frame those actions as deliberate attempts to cause harm. This involves attributing negative motives to the opponent's behavior. For example, if the opponent proposes a new policy, it can be framed as a move to benefit only the elite while harming ordinary citizens. By suggesting that the opponent is acting out of selfishness, greed, or even malice, the propagandist ensures that their actions are seen as part of a larger, sinister agenda. The opponent is not just misguided; they are actively working against the interests of the people.

Creating associations is a technique that links the opponent to already existing fears, prejudices, or negative concepts. For example, associating the opponent with foreign enemies, controversial ideologies, or criminal behavior creates an immediate negative connection in the minds of the audience. This technique leverages existing biases and emotions to create a sense of distrust and animosity. Visuals, stories, and even indirect hints can be used to make these associations. The more often the opponent is mentioned in the same context as something the audience fears or dislikes, the stronger the association becomes.

Using fear-driven language is essential for amplifying the perceived threat. Words like "danger," "threat," "collapse," and "crisis" evoke a sense of urgency and make the audience feel that immediate action is necessary. The language used should make the opponent's actions seem reckless and dangerous, and their influence as something that must be stopped at all costs. The goal is to create a sense of imminent threat, so that the audience feels compelled to act against the opponent. Fear-driven language bypasses rational analysis, triggering emotional responses that lead the audience to accept the enemy narrative without question.

Simplifying complex issues is also important in crafting an enemy narrative. Complex social, political, or economic problems are often difficult for people to fully understand, and the propagandist can take advantage of this by simplifying these issues and attributing them to the actions of the opponent. For example, economic hardship can be blamed on the opponent's policies, regardless of the actual underlying factors. This simplification makes it easier for the audience to understand who is to blame, creating a direct link between the problem and the enemy. The more straightforward the narrative, the more likely it is to resonate with the audience.

Utilizing scapegoating is another powerful technique. Scapegoating involves blaming the opponent for issues that the audience is already frustrated or anxious about. By positioning the opponent as the cause of societal problems—whether it is unemployment, crime, or cultural decline—the propagandist gives the audience a tangible target for their anger. This provides a sense of relief, as the audience now has a clear source of blame for their hardships. Scapegoating is effective because it simplifies the world into good versus evil, giving people a clear enemy to oppose.

Appealing to group identity is crucial for building a narrative that resonates deeply. The propagandist must position the opponent as a threat to the group's identity, values, and way of life. By creating an "us versus them" dynamic, the audience is made to feel that their entire community is under threat from the opponent. This taps into the powerful need for belonging and protection of the in-group, making the audience more likely to unite against the perceived enemy. The propagandist should emphasize that the opponent is fundamentally different—someone who does not share the same values, beliefs, or loyalties as the rest of the group.

Finally, **repetition** is the cornerstone of an effective enemy narrative. No matter how powerful the message, it needs to be repeated consistently across multiple channels to take root. The same story, labels, associations, and fear-driven messages must be broadcast over and over again, using different formats and media to reach the widest possible audience. Repetition creates familiarity, and familiarity breeds acceptance. The more often the audience hears the message, the more likely they are to accept it as the truth. Consistent repetition ensures that the enemy narrative becomes part of the public consciousness, shaping how people think and feel about the opponent.

Creating an enemy narrative is about constructing a cohesive and emotionally resonant story that portrays the opponent as a clear and present danger. Through selective storytelling, labeling, framing intentions, creating associations, using fear-driven language, simplifying issues, scapegoating, appealing to group identity, and relentless repetition, the propagandist can turn an opponent into a feared and hated enemy. These practical techniques work together to shape perception, rally support, and mobilize collective action against the perceived threat, ensuring that the enemy narrative takes hold and drives the desired response from the audience.

Part 2: Enemies of Faith: How Religion Constructs and Sustains the Idea of Opposition

Throughout history, religion has been one of the most powerful forces for uniting people around shared values, beliefs, and practices. However, unity often requires a common adversary—an "enemy" that threatens the purity and sanctity of the faith. By framing ideological opposition as a direct threat to the core tenets of a religion, religious leaders have long been able to rally their followers, instilling loyalty and devotion through the use of fear and the construction of clear boundaries between believers and "outsiders."

The construction of enemies of faith is not merely a matter of identifying those who hold different beliefs. It is a deliberate process of turning differing ideologies into existential threats, creating a narrative in which the survival of the faith depends on resisting these opposing forces. This narrative is bolstered by the authority of religious doctrine, which defines the boundaries of acceptable beliefs and behavior. Those who fall outside these boundaries are labeled as enemies—individuals or groups whose very existence is a challenge to the faith and the community of believers.

Fear has always played a central role in cultivating loyalty and maintaining control within religious groups. By emphasizing the dangers posed by those who hold differing views, religious leaders can unite their followers around a common cause—defending the faith from perceived threats. This fear-driven unity often leads to the scapegoating of individuals or groups, turning them into symbols of everything that must be resisted. Throughout history, religious conflicts have been fueled by such narratives, where the perceived threat to the faith has justified violence, persecution, and exclusion.

In modern times, religious leaders continue to identify new "threats to faith" in response to cultural shifts and changes in societal norms. The rise of secularism, scientific advancements, and evolving social values have all been framed as threats to religious orthodoxy. By exploiting these cultural shifts and using technology to amplify the enemy narrative, religious leaders are able to maintain a sense of urgency and defensiveness among their followers. Social media, in particular, has become a powerful tool for spreading messages of fear and distrust, ensuring that the perceived threat remains at the forefront of the community's consciousness.

This part of the book will explore how religious leaders construct and sustain the idea of ideological opposition as an existential threat to the faith. It will delve into the techniques used to cultivate loyalty through fear, drawing on historical and modern examples of religious conflicts and scapegoating. Practical guidance will be provided for religious leaders seeking to create compelling adversaries—whether they are ideologies, cultural movements, or individuals—and strategies for using propaganda to sustain followers' loyalty. By understanding the role of enemies in religious narratives, one can gain insight into how faith communities are shaped, maintained, and mobilized in the face of perceived threats.

Chapter 5: Constructing the Enemy of Faith: Framing Ideological Opposition as a Threat

Religion has always been more than a system of beliefs; it is a powerful force for community building, identity formation, and social cohesion. To maintain unity and ensure adherence to doctrine, religious leaders often construct ideological opposition as a direct threat to the faith. The process of framing those with differing beliefs as enemies serves to solidify the boundaries of the community, creating a clear distinction between "us"—the righteous, the faithful—and "them"—the outsiders, the threat. This technique has been used throughout history to rally followers, eliminate dissent, and maintain the purity of the faith.

Religious leaders construct enemies of faith by highlighting how opposing beliefs or practices contradict the core teachings of their religion. These ideological opponents are not simply portrayed as misguided individuals but as active threats to the well-being of the entire community. By emphasizing the dangers that these opposing views pose, leaders are able to create an atmosphere of urgency and defensiveness. The narrative becomes one of survival—where the continued existence of the faith is contingent upon resisting and overcoming these adversaries.

Doctrinal authority plays a crucial role in the process of constructing enemies of faith. Religious texts, interpretations, and authoritative teachings are used to define what is acceptable and what is not, creating a framework for determining who belongs and who does not. Those who fall outside these boundaries are labeled as "outsiders" or even enemies, positioning them as fundamentally opposed to the values and truths of the faith. The use of doctrine not only legitimizes this exclusion but also gives it a sense of divine sanction, making it difficult for followers to question or challenge the narrative.

The framing of ideological opposition as a threat serves multiple purposes. It reinforces the authority of religious leaders by presenting them as defenders of the faith, strengthens group identity by defining clear boundaries, and motivates followers to take action against perceived enemies. This chapter will explore how religious leaders use their authority to construct enemies of faith, examining both historical and modern examples. It will also delve into the impact of doctrinal authority in creating "outsiders" and how these narratives shape the way faith communities perceive and respond to ideological opposition. By understanding these dynamics, one can see how the construction of enemies serves to maintain control, foster unity, and protect the core tenets of the faith.

Defining the Adversary: How Religious Leaders Construct Enemies of Faith

RELIGIOUS LEADERS HAVE long understood that defining an enemy is a powerful way to unify followers, establish clear boundaries, and protect the integrity of the faith. Constructing an "enemy of faith" involves framing certain individuals, groups, or ideologies as existential threats to the religion's core values and the community's spiritual well-being. This process requires a combination of rhetoric, selective interpretation of doctrine, and strategic framing to ensure that these enemies are perceived as dangerous, immoral, and fundamentally opposed to the values of the faith.

One of the primary ways religious leaders construct enemies of faith is by framing ideological differences as moral failings. This involves taking opposing beliefs or practices and portraying them as inherently evil or corrupt. For example, an ideology that promotes secularism or alternative moral perspectives might be presented as an attack on divine truth, undermining the fundamental teachings of the religion. By positioning these ideologies as a moral threat, religious leaders can mobilize their followers to defend the faith, creating a sense of duty and righteousness in opposing the enemy.

Selective interpretation of religious texts also plays a crucial role in constructing enemies of faith. Religious doctrines are often open to interpretation, and leaders can emphasize certain passages or reinterpret teachings to support the idea that specific beliefs or groups are enemies. By highlighting verses or teachings that speak against particular behaviors or ideologies, religious leaders can lend divine authority to the idea of opposition. This makes it difficult for followers to question the narrative, as it is presented not as a matter of opinion but as an unquestionable aspect of the faith itself.

The process of constructing enemies of faith often involves **dehumanization**—framing the enemy as fundamentally different, immoral, or subhuman. By emphasizing the differences between the in-group (the faithful) and the out-group (the enemy), leaders create a sense of "us versus them" that strengthens group identity. The enemy is portrayed as someone who threatens not only the community's beliefs but also their way of life, security, and relationship with the divine. Dehumanization makes it easier for followers to justify harsh measures against the enemy, whether it is exclusion, persecution, or even violence, as these individuals are seen as beyond redemption.

Religious leaders also use **scapegoating** as a tactic for constructing enemies of faith. When a community faces hardship or challenges, it is often easier to attribute these problems to an external enemy rather than internal issues. By blaming societal or spiritual problems on a specific group or ideology, leaders provide their followers with a clear target for their frustrations. This tactic not only unites the community against a common adversary but also deflects blame away from internal flaws or leadership failures, preserving the authority and cohesion of the group.

Emotional appeals are another important aspect of constructing enemies of faith. By using rhetoric that evokes fear, anger, or disgust, religious leaders can create an emotional response that reinforces the idea of the enemy as a threat. Describing the enemy as "wicked," "dangerous," or "corrupting" instills a sense of fear, which can then be channeled into loyalty and action. The more emotional the narrative, the more deeply it resonates with followers, making the enemy narrative a powerful tool for maintaining control and influence.

Religious rituals and symbols can also be used to reinforce the enemy narrative. Leaders may incorporate prayers, sermons, or rituals that emphasize the struggle against the enemy, framing it as a spiritual battle that every believer must participate in. Symbols that represent the enemy—whether it is imagery, slogans, or icons—can be used to create a constant reminder of the threat, ensuring that the sense of opposition remains present in the daily lives of followers. This ongoing reinforcement keeps the idea of the enemy alive and ensures that the community remains vigilant.

Ultimately, constructing enemies of faith is about maintaining the cohesion and purity of the religious community. By defining an adversary, leaders create a clear boundary between what is acceptable and what is not, establishing themselves as the defenders of the faith and the community. The enemy narrative serves as a powerful tool for controlling followers, instilling loyalty, and motivating action, ensuring that the community remains united in the face of both real and perceived threats. Through moral framing, doctrinal authority, dehumanization, scapegoating, emotional appeals, and symbolic reinforcement, religious leaders can effectively construct enemies of faith and use them to strengthen their influence over their followers.

Defining Boundaries: The Impact of Doctrinal Authority on Creating "Outsiders"

DOCTRINAL AUTHORITY is one of the most powerful tools in constructing and maintaining the boundaries of a religious community. By establishing what is true, acceptable, and righteous, religious doctrines define who belongs and who does not—creating clear distinctions between those who are considered faithful and those who fall outside of that category. This process of defining boundaries is instrumental in creating "outsiders," individuals or groups who are seen as a threat to the integrity of the faith and community. The impact of doctrinal authority on creating outsiders is profound, as it not only influences the beliefs and behaviors of followers but also shapes the way they view those who are different.

Doctrinal authority is grounded in sacred texts, religious teachings, and the interpretations of recognized leaders. When a particular belief or practice is deemed heretical or contrary to the core teachings of the faith, those who hold to it are automatically classified as outsiders. This categorization is not merely an intellectual distinction; it is a moral and spiritual one. By defining certain beliefs as incompatible with the faith, doctrinal authority positions those who hold them as fundamentally opposed to the community's values. This makes outsiders not just different, but dangerous—individuals who must be resisted, shunned, or even eliminated to protect the purity of the faith.

The process of creating outsiders often begins with the interpretation of religious texts. Religious doctrines are complex, and their teachings can be interpreted in different ways depending on the context and the objectives of those in power. Religious leaders may emphasize certain passages over others, using these interpretations to justify the exclusion of specific groups or ideas. By presenting their interpretation as the only true understanding of the doctrine, leaders wield the authority to determine who is in alignment with the faith and who is not. This authority gives their pronouncements a sense of divine legitimacy, making it difficult for followers to question or challenge the exclusion of outsiders.

In many cases, doctrinal authority is used to define the boundaries of acceptable behavior and belief, creating a set of norms that followers must adhere to. Those who deviate from these norms are labeled as outsiders, often with severe consequences. This can include those who adopt different religious practices, hold divergent theological views, or simply question the authority of religious leaders. By defining these individuals as enemies of the faith, doctrinal authority ensures that any deviation is met with resistance and condemnation. The fear of being labeled an outsider serves as a powerful deterrent, encouraging conformity and discouraging dissent within the community.

Doctrinal authority also plays a crucial role in shaping the narrative around outsiders. By framing those who fall outside the boundaries of the faith as morally corrupt, spiritually lost, or even evil, leaders create a sense of fear and distrust. This narrative serves to dehumanize outsiders, making it easier for followers to justify treating them with suspicion, hostility, or even violence. The use of language that positions outsiders as inherently flawed or dangerous reinforces the idea that they are a threat to the community's spiritual well-being, further solidifying the boundary between "us" and "them."

The creation of outsiders is not only about exclusion but also about strengthening the identity of the in-group. By defining who does not belong, doctrinal authority helps to clarify what it means to be a true member of the faith. The presence of outsiders serves as a contrast, highlighting the virtues and values of those who are faithful. This process reinforces group cohesion and loyalty, as followers are reminded of the importance of adhering to the teachings that set them apart from those who are seen as enemies. The existence of outsiders creates a sense of solidarity among followers, as they rally together to protect their shared beliefs and values.

The impact of doctrinal authority on creating outsiders can be seen throughout history in instances of persecution, excommunication, and religious conflict. Whether it is the targeting of heretics during the Inquisition, the exclusion of dissenting sects, or the demonization of those who embrace different religious traditions, the power of doctrinal authority to define and exclude has had profound consequences for individuals and communities. By positioning outsiders as threats to the faith, religious leaders have justified actions ranging from social ostracism to violent persecution, all in the name of protecting the integrity of the community.

Ultimately, the use of doctrinal authority to create outsiders is a way for religious leaders to maintain control, enforce conformity, and protect the boundaries of their community. By defining what is true and who belongs, they ensure that their followers remain loyal, united, and committed to the defense of the faith. The impact of this process goes beyond mere exclusion; it shapes the way followers perceive the world, reinforcing a worldview in which the faithful are constantly under threat from those who do not share their beliefs. Through the power of doctrine, religious leaders can create a clear and compelling enemy narrative, one that keeps followers vigilant, united, and loyal to the cause.

Chapter 6: Binding Through Fear: Techniques for Uniting Followers in Faith

Fear has long been a powerful tool for uniting people, especially within religious communities. When faced with a common threat, individuals are more likely to rally together, putting aside their differences to protect what they hold sacred. Religious leaders have often leveraged this instinct by using fear as a means to cultivate loyalty and strengthen the bonds among their followers. By presenting ideological, cultural, or even existential threats, leaders create a sense of urgency and necessity that drives collective action and reinforces the group's identity.

The process of using fear to unite followers involves identifying an enemy—whether it is an external group, a divergent ideology, or a perceived cultural shift—and framing it as an immediate danger to the faith and the community. This narrative of threat generates a shared fear that binds followers together, creating a sense of solidarity against a common adversary. The fear of losing one's values, traditions, or even divine favor compels followers to support their leaders without question, as they are positioned as protectors against the encroaching threat.

Scapegoating is another common technique used to channel fear and anxiety. By placing blame for the community's problems on a specific individual or group, religious leaders provide their followers with a clear target for their anger and frustrations. Scapegoating simplifies complex issues, offering a convenient explanation for suffering, and creates a tangible enemy that must be opposed. This dynamic not only strengthens the unity of the in-group but also serves to divert attention away from any internal issues or dissent within the community.

Throughout history, many religious conflicts have been fueled by fear-driven narratives and scapegoating. The fear of heresy, the threat of losing cultural or spiritual identity, and the desire to maintain doctrinal purity have all been used to justify conflicts, persecution, and exclusion. These historical examples provide valuable lessons on how fear can be cultivated and weaponized to mobilize followers, solidify group loyalty, and eliminate perceived threats.

This chapter will explore the techniques religious leaders use to cultivate loyalty through fear, focusing on how threats are framed and how scapegoating is employed to create a clear enemy. It will also include case studies of historical religious conflicts where fear played a central role in uniting followers and justifying extreme actions. By understanding these techniques, it becomes clear how fear can be harnessed to build cohesion, loyalty, and obedience within a religious community, even at the cost of vilifying and persecuting others.

Uniting Through Fear: Techniques for Creating a Cohesive Community

FEAR IS A POTENT FORCE for uniting individuals, particularly within religious communities, where shared beliefs and the desire for collective security are paramount. By leveraging fear, religious leaders can create a sense of urgency and vulnerability that compels followers to come together in defense of their faith and community. The construction of an external threat—whether it is a perceived ideological enemy, a cultural change, or an impending crisis—serves as a catalyst for loyalty, solidarity, and unquestioning support. The following techniques are commonly used to harness fear and use it as a powerful unifying tool.

The first technique is **framing an existential threat**. Religious leaders often present challenges or opposing ideologies as existential threats to the faith, emphasizing that the community's survival is at stake. This framing transforms what might otherwise be seen as a mere difference of opinion into an urgent matter of life and death. By portraying the enemy as a threat to the very essence of the community's identity, leaders create an atmosphere of crisis that demands immediate and unified action. Followers are more likely to rally together when they believe their way of life or their relationship with the divine is in jeopardy.

Another powerful technique is **demonizing the enemy**. By framing those outside the faith as inherently evil or morally corrupt, religious leaders instill fear and distrust among their followers. This process of demonization dehumanizes the enemy, portraying them as a force of darkness that must be resisted at all costs. The use of emotive language—such as calling the enemy "wicked," "heretical," or "an abomination"—evokes strong emotional responses, reinforcing the need for unity against the perceived threat. By creating a stark contrast between the "righteous" followers and the "evil" enemy, religious leaders foster an "us versus them" mentality that strengthens group cohesion.

Scapegoating is another technique that is frequently used to unite followers through fear. When a community faces challenges—such as economic hardship, social unrest, or even natural disasters—leaders may blame these problems on an external enemy or an internal group that deviates from the accepted norms. By attributing the community's suffering to the actions of a scapegoat, leaders provide a simple explanation for complex issues, giving followers a target for their anger and frustrations. This process not only unites the community against a common adversary but also diverts attention away from any potential shortcomings of the leadership itself.

Exaggeration and hyperbole are key tools for amplifying fear and creating a sense of urgency. Religious leaders may take a minor threat or difference and present it as a major crisis that requires immediate action. By using hyperbolic language—such as "the end of our faith," "a complete moral collapse," or "an attack on everything we hold sacred"—leaders can amplify the perceived danger and convince followers that there is no time for debate or hesitation. This sense of urgency prevents rational deliberation and compels followers to act quickly and decisively in defense of their beliefs.

Rituals and symbols are also effective in reinforcing fear and uniting followers. By incorporating rituals that emphasize the community's struggle against the enemy—such as prayers for protection, sermons about resisting evil, or symbolic acts of defiance—leaders create a shared experience that binds followers together. Symbols that represent the enemy or the threat they pose can also be used to evoke fear and remind followers of the need for vigilance. These rituals and symbols create a sense of collective purpose, reinforcing the idea that the community must stand together against the threat.

The use of **fear-based narratives** is another effective technique for uniting followers. Leaders craft stories that highlight the dangers posed by the enemy, often using anecdotal evidence or personal testimonies to make the threat feel real and immediate. These narratives may include accounts of individuals who have "fallen victim" to the enemy's influence or stories of communities that have suffered as a result of straying from the faith. By personalizing the threat, leaders create an emotional connection that resonates deeply with followers, making the fear more tangible and the need for unity more pressing.

Isolation from external influences is a tactic used to ensure that the fear-driven narrative remains uncontested. By discouraging followers from engaging with outside ideas or individuals who may challenge the narrative, leaders create an environment where fear is constantly reinforced. Followers are instructed to avoid contact with those who hold opposing views, and any attempt to question the enemy narrative is framed as dangerous or sinful. This isolation prevents followers from encountering alternative perspectives, ensuring that the fear remains focused on the constructed enemy and that loyalty to the community remains unchallenged.

Finally, **repetition** is crucial for ensuring that the message of fear takes hold and remains effective. The perceived threat must be mentioned consistently—during sermons, in religious texts, through social media, and in everyday conversations. By repeating the same warnings and emphasizing the same dangers, leaders ensure that fear becomes a part of the followers' daily consciousness. This repetition not only reinforces the belief in the threat but also keeps the community united in their shared anxiety and determination to protect the faith.

By using these techniques—framing existential threats, demonizing the enemy, scapegoating, exaggeration, rituals and symbols, fear-based narratives, isolation, and repetition—religious leaders can effectively use fear to unite followers and strengthen the bonds of the community. Fear serves as a powerful motivator, driving followers to act in defense of their faith and creating a sense of solidarity that is difficult to achieve through other means. When followers believe that they are facing an imminent and dangerous threat, they are more likely to put aside internal differences, support their leaders, and work together in pursuit of a common cause.

Historical Lessons: Case Studies of Religious Conflicts and Scapegoating

RELIGIOUS CONFLICTS throughout history have often been fueled by scapegoating—assigning blame for societal problems to a particular group, which then becomes the target of collective fear and hostility. This process of identifying and vilifying an enemy serves to strengthen group cohesion and validate the authority of religious leaders by uniting followers against a perceived threat. Examining historical case studies reveals how scapegoating has been used to justify persecution, consolidate power, and maintain social control, often with devastating consequences.

One prominent example of scapegoating in religious conflicts is the **Spanish Inquisition**. During the late 15th century, the Spanish monarchy, with the backing of the Catholic Church, launched the Inquisition to root out heresy and enforce religious conformity. Jews and Muslims, along with conversos (those who had converted to Christianity but were suspected of secretly practicing their former faith), were scapegoated as threats to the purity of the Christian faith and the stability of the kingdom. The Inquisition framed these groups as enemies who were undermining the true faith and corrupting society from within. This narrative of fear allowed the Church to justify the persecution, imprisonment, and execution of thousands of individuals, while also reinforcing the authority of the Church and the monarchy. The systematic scapegoating of religious minorities not only united the Christian population in their shared fear of heresy but also served as a powerful tool for consolidating political and religious power.

Another example of religious scapegoating is the **witch hunts** of early modern Europe, particularly during the 16th and 17th centuries. During this period, the Church and state authorities blamed witches for a wide range of societal problems, including failed crops, plagues, and other misfortunes. Women, in particular, were targeted and scapegoated as witches, accused of making pacts with the devil and bringing harm to their communities. This scapegoating served multiple purposes: it provided an explanation for the community's suffering, it offered an outlet for social tensions, and it reinforced the moral authority of religious leaders, who positioned themselves as protectors against the forces of evil. The fear-driven narrative of witchcraft created a sense of urgency and paranoia, leading to the torture, execution, and ostracism of thousands of innocent people, all in the name of defending the community from an imagined threat.

A more recent example of scapegoating in a religious conflict can be seen in the **Rwandan Genocide** of 1994. While the conflict had deep historical and political roots, religious narratives played a significant role in fueling hatred and violence. The Hutu majority used propaganda to portray the Tutsi minority as dangerous and subhuman, referring to them as "cockroaches" and enemies of the Rwandan nation. Religious leaders, including some within the Christian Church, either supported this narrative or remained silent, allowing the message of hatred to spread unchallenged. The use of fear and dehumanizing language created an environment where the Hutu population felt justified in committing acts of mass violence against their Tutsi neighbors. The scapegoating of the Tutsi as enemies of the nation and threats to social stability led to one of the most horrific genocides of the 20th century, with over 800,000 people killed in a matter of months.

The **Crusades** provide yet another example of how religious conflicts have been fueled by scapegoating. Beginning in the late 11th century, the Catholic Church called on Christians to take up arms and reclaim the Holy Land from Muslim control. Muslims were portrayed as infidels and enemies of Christendom, and the call to Crusade was framed as a sacred duty to defend the faith from an existential threat. The scapegoating of Muslims as enemies of Christianity served to unify European Christians across political and cultural divides, creating a sense of common purpose. The fear-driven narrative of an enemy threatening the holy sites of Christianity allowed the Church to mobilize large armies, justify violence, and extend its influence. The Crusades led to centuries of conflict, fueled by a narrative of religious opposition and the scapegoating of those who were portrayed as a threat to the Christian world.

During the **Protestant Reformation** in the 16th century, both the Catholic Church and Protestant reformers used scapegoating to rally their followers and delegitimize their opponents. The Catholic Church labeled Protestant reformers as heretics and enemies of the true faith, blaming them for causing division and chaos within Christendom. Conversely, Protestant leaders scapegoated the Catholic Church as corrupt and morally bankrupt, accusing it of leading believers away from true Christian teachings. This mutual scapegoating led to widespread religious conflicts, including wars, persecutions, and executions, as both sides sought to eliminate what they saw as a threat to the integrity of their faith. The use of fear and scapegoating created a climate of hostility and division, with each side viewing the other as an existential danger that had to be opposed at all costs.

These historical case studies illustrate the destructive power of scapegoating in religious conflicts. By identifying a specific group as the cause of societal problems or as a threat to the faith, religious leaders can create a compelling enemy narrative that unites followers and justifies extreme actions. The process of scapegoating simplifies complex issues, providing a clear target for fear and anger, while also reinforcing the authority of religious leaders as defenders of the community. The use of fear, dehumanization, and moral framing in these conflicts reveals how effective scapegoating can be in mobilizing followers and maintaining control, even at the cost of widespread suffering and injustice.

The lessons from these case studies are clear: scapegoating can be a powerful tool for uniting followers and defending religious authority, but it comes with significant ethical and moral consequences. The creation of an enemy through scapegoating can lead to persecution, violence, and the destruction of innocent lives, all in the name of defending the faith. Understanding these historical examples allows us to see the dangers of using fear and scapegoating as tools for social control and serves as a reminder of the importance of empathy, critical thinking, and resisting the temptation to simplify complex issues by blaming others.

Chapter 7: The Modern Adversary: Exploiting Cultural Shifts and Amplifying Threats

In the contemporary world, religious leaders face new challenges that come from evolving cultural norms, technological advancements, and the increasing influence of secularism. These changes can be perceived as threats to traditional values and beliefs, creating an opportunity for religious leaders to frame these modern shifts as dangers that must be resisted. By identifying these cultural shifts and presenting them as existential threats to the faith, leaders can galvanize their followers, reinforcing the importance of adhering to established doctrines and resisting the influence of the outside world.

Modern cultural shifts, such as the growing acceptance of diverse lifestyles, changing family dynamics, and the rise of scientific and secular worldviews, often clash with traditional religious teachings. Religious leaders can exploit these shifts by positioning them as attacks on the core tenets of the faith. This involves identifying specific changes—such as new laws that contradict religious doctrines or cultural trends that challenge traditional morality—and framing them as evidence of a broader assault on the community's values. The goal is to create a sense of crisis, where the survival of the faith depends on standing firm against these external influences.

The advent of technology has made it easier than ever for religious leaders to amplify the idea of an enemy and spread their message to a wider audience. Social media platforms, messaging apps, and online forums allow for the rapid dissemination of fear-driven narratives, reaching followers directly and repeatedly. By leveraging these technologies, religious leaders can create a constant flow of messages that emphasize the dangers posed by modern cultural shifts, ensuring that the perceived threat remains at the forefront of their followers' minds. This continuous exposure reinforces the idea that the faith is under attack and that unity is needed to protect it.

Technology also enables religious leaders to target specific audiences with tailored messages. Algorithms can be used to amplify content that resonates with certain demographics, ensuring that the message reaches those who are most likely to respond. This allows for a more focused approach to enemy creation, where different aspects of modern cultural shifts are emphasized based on the concerns and values of particular groups within the community. By tailoring the message in this way, leaders can strengthen the loyalty of their followers and ensure that the enemy narrative is deeply embedded in their worldview.

This chapter will examine how religious leaders target modern "threats to faith" by exploiting cultural shifts and using technology to amplify the idea of an enemy. It will explore the ways in which cultural changes are framed as attacks on traditional values and how technology is harnessed to spread fear-driven messages and create a sense of urgency. By understanding these techniques, one can see how religious leaders adapt their strategies to address contemporary challenges, maintaining control and loyalty in an increasingly connected and evolving world.

Exploiting Modern Changes: Identifying and Leveraging Cultural Shifts as Threats

AS SOCIETIES EVOLVE, cultural shifts bring about new values, norms, and ideas that may challenge established religious doctrines. Religious leaders often identify these shifts as potential threats to their faith and leverage them to create narratives that reinforce group loyalty, heighten fear, and rally followers against perceived dangers. By framing modern cultural changes as existential threats, leaders can mobilize their communities to resist what they see as attacks on their core beliefs, thus ensuring their followers remain committed and united in defense of the faith.

The first step in exploiting cultural shifts is **identifying changes that contradict traditional religious values**. These changes can include increased acceptance of diverse lifestyles, shifts in family structures, advancements in science and technology, or rising secularism. Leaders must carefully observe the cultural landscape, pinpointing emerging trends that could be positioned as challenges to the community's moral framework. For example, the growing acceptance of LGBTQ+ rights and gender equality can be portrayed as undermining traditional family values, thus threatening the religious teachings on marriage and gender roles. By framing these changes as a fundamental threat to the moral order, leaders create a sense of urgency and a need to protect the community from losing its spiritual identity.

Once the cultural shifts have been identified, **framing them as direct attacks on religious beliefs** is essential for constructing a compelling enemy narrative. Leaders often describe these changes using fear-driven language, positioning them as deliberate efforts to erode the values that the community holds sacred. This framing transforms cultural changes from mere differences of opinion into existential threats that require an active response. By emphasizing that these shifts are part of a broader agenda to secularize society, weaken religious influence, or promote immorality, leaders ensure that followers perceive the threat as immediate and dangerous. The rhetoric of "defending the faith" and "standing against corruption" creates a powerful emotional connection that binds the community together.

Exaggeration and hyperbole are also commonly used to amplify the perceived threat of modern cultural changes. By presenting these shifts as catastrophic and suggesting that they will lead to the "collapse of society" or the "end of our values," leaders ensure that the audience feels a strong sense of urgency. This exaggeration prevents followers from viewing these changes as natural or inevitable and instead frames them as crises that must be resisted. The sense of urgency created by hyperbole compels followers to act, ensuring that they align themselves with the leadership in opposing the perceived threat.

Selective storytelling is another key technique used to exploit modern cultural shifts. Religious leaders may highlight specific incidents or examples that align with the narrative they wish to promote while ignoring counterexamples. For instance, they might point to cases where societal acceptance of a particular behavior led to negative outcomes, using these examples to argue that the entire cultural shift is inherently dangerous. By presenting these stories in sermons, publications, and social media, leaders can reinforce the narrative that the changes pose a real and present danger to the community. This selective use of evidence helps to make the threat feel tangible and immediate.

The use of **religious doctrine** to frame cultural shifts as heretical or sinful is another effective tactic. By referencing sacred texts or established teachings that explicitly condemn the changes taking place in broader society, religious leaders lend divine authority to their arguments. This approach not only positions the cultural shifts as morally wrong but also frames them as a direct challenge to divine will. Followers are thus encouraged to resist these changes not just for the sake of their community but as a matter of spiritual duty. The invocation of doctrine serves to make the resistance to cultural shifts a sacred obligation, deepening the emotional commitment of followers.

Targeting the fear of losing community identity is also critical. Cultural shifts often bring about changes in social norms and practices that can lead to a perceived dilution of the community's unique identity. Religious leaders exploit this fear by suggesting that embracing or even tolerating these shifts will lead to the erosion of their distinct way of life. This tactic plays on followers' anxieties about losing their cultural heritage, their connection to their ancestors, and their unique religious practices. By emphasizing that the survival of the community's identity is at stake, leaders motivate followers to resist any influence that might bring about unwanted changes.

In addition, **mobilizing against perceived external enemies** is an effective way to unite followers in opposition to cultural shifts. Leaders may frame those advocating for these changes—whether they are activists, government bodies, or even members of the community—as enemies of the faith. These individuals or groups are portrayed as agents of a broader agenda designed to undermine the community's values. This externalization of the threat makes it easier for followers to direct their fear and hostility outward, rallying against a clear enemy rather than questioning the changes themselves. By positioning advocates of cultural shifts as enemies, leaders create a rallying point that strengthens group solidarity.

To exploit modern cultural shifts effectively, religious leaders must also **control the narrative through strategic use of media and communication channels**. Social media, in particular, has become a powerful tool for spreading fear-driven narratives about cultural changes. Leaders can use platforms such as Facebook, Twitter, and messaging apps to disseminate content that highlights the dangers of cultural shifts, amplifies the perceived threat, and reinforces the message of resistance. The viral nature of social media ensures that these narratives reach a wide audience, and the use of images, videos, and testimonials can make the message even more impactful. By controlling the narrative and ensuring that followers are constantly exposed to messages that reinforce the enemy narrative, leaders can maintain a sense of urgency and vigilance.

Repetition is also crucial for ensuring that the message takes root. The narrative that cultural shifts are a threat to the faith must be repeated consistently across various platforms—during sermons, in publications, on social media, and in community gatherings. The constant repetition of the same warnings and messages ensures that the perceived threat remains top of mind for followers. This ongoing reinforcement helps to ingrain the belief that cultural shifts must be resisted, making the enemy narrative an integral part of the community's worldview.

By identifying modern cultural shifts and framing them as existential threats to the faith, religious leaders can exploit these changes to create compelling enemy narratives that resonate with their followers. Through framing, exaggeration, selective storytelling, doctrinal authority, targeting identity fears, mobilizing against external enemies, media control, and repetition, leaders can ensure that their communities remain united, loyal, and resistant to outside influences. These techniques allow religious leaders to maintain their influence and protect their communities from changes that they perceive as dangerous to their core values and identity.

Digital Warfare: Using Technology to Amplify the Idea of an Enemy

IN THE MODERN AGE, technology has become an indispensable tool for amplifying narratives, shaping public perception, and mobilizing followers. Religious leaders and organizations have harnessed the power of digital platforms to spread their messages, including the idea of a common enemy. By utilizing social media, messaging apps, websites, and other digital tools, leaders can create an omnipresent sense of threat that reinforces group identity and solidifies loyalty among their followers. This amplification of the enemy narrative is not only about increasing reach but also about making the perceived threat feel immediate, real, and personal.

The most powerful tool for amplifying the idea of an enemy is **social media**. Platforms like Facebook, Twitter, Instagram, and YouTube allow for the rapid dissemination of content that frames certain individuals, groups, or ideologies as threats. Religious leaders can create posts, videos, and live streams that use fear-driven language and emotive visuals to evoke strong emotional responses. By repeatedly sharing content that portrays the enemy in a negative light, leaders can create a sense of urgency and mobilize followers to take action. Social media also provides an opportunity for direct engagement, allowing leaders to interact with followers, address their concerns, and reinforce the idea of the enemy through personal communication.

Algorithms play a significant role in amplifying the enemy narrative on social media. Platforms use algorithms to promote content that generates engagement—likes, shares, comments—and content that evokes strong emotions is more likely to go viral. Religious leaders can take advantage of these algorithms by creating highly emotive and polarizing content that elicits fear, anger, or a sense of injustice. As followers engage with this content, it reaches a wider audience, creating a feedback loop where the enemy narrative is continuously amplified. This amplification ensures that the idea of the enemy becomes deeply ingrained in the minds of the followers and that it dominates their digital environment.

Targeted advertising is another effective way to amplify the enemy narrative. Social media platforms allow for precise targeting based on demographics, interests, and behaviors. Religious leaders can use these tools to reach specific segments of their audience with tailored messages that emphasize the threat posed by the enemy. For example, younger followers might receive content that frames the enemy as a threat to their future, while older followers might see messages emphasizing the loss of traditional values. By tailoring the message to resonate with different audiences, leaders can ensure that the fear-driven narrative is effective across various demographics.

Messaging apps such as WhatsApp, Telegram, and Signal are also valuable tools for spreading the enemy narrative. These apps allow for private, encrypted communication, making them ideal for sharing messages that might be considered controversial or inflammatory. Leaders can use group chats to disseminate content that frames the enemy as a threat, ensuring that followers receive the message directly and without interference. The closed nature of these groups also creates an echo chamber where the enemy narrative is reinforced, as followers are exposed only to information that aligns with the group's beliefs. This lack of exposure to opposing viewpoints makes the idea of the enemy feel even more credible and urgent.

Content creation is another important aspect of using technology to amplify the idea of an enemy. Blogs, podcasts, and videos can be used to create detailed narratives that explain why the enemy is a threat and what followers must do to resist. These longer formats allow leaders to provide "evidence" of the enemy's actions, using anecdotal stories, selective data, and religious teachings to build a compelling case. By creating a wide range of content—articles, documentaries, interviews—leaders can ensure that followers have access to a steady stream of information that reinforces the enemy narrative. This content can then be shared across social media, messaging apps, and websites, maximizing its reach and impact.

Visual content is particularly effective in amplifying the idea of an enemy. Images and videos evoke strong emotional reactions and can convey a sense of threat more powerfully than words alone. Religious leaders can use visual content to create a stark contrast between the community and the enemy, emphasizing the danger posed by those who fall outside the group. Images that depict chaos, destruction, or moral decay can be used to represent the enemy, while contrasting visuals of peace, unity, and prosperity are used to represent the faithful community. This visual juxtaposition reinforces the idea that the enemy is a threat that must be opposed to protect the community's way of life.

Memes are another digital tool that can be used to spread the enemy narrative. Memes are easily shareable, often humorous images or videos that convey a message in a simple and impactful way. Religious leaders and their followers can use memes to mock or demonize the enemy, making the idea of opposition more appealing and accessible, especially to younger audiences. Memes are effective because they condense complex ideas into simple, emotionally charged visuals that are easy to understand and share. The viral nature of memes ensures that the enemy narrative reaches a wide audience, further amplifying the sense of threat.

Online communities and forums also play a role in amplifying the idea of an enemy. Platforms like Reddit, Discord, and other online forums allow followers to discuss the enemy narrative, share personal experiences, and reinforce each other's beliefs. These communities create a sense of solidarity and shared purpose, as followers feel that they are part of a larger movement resisting a common threat. The more followers engage with these communities, the more they are exposed to content that reinforces the enemy narrative, creating a cycle of confirmation and amplification.

Finally, **data analytics** can be used to measure the effectiveness of the enemy narrative and adjust the messaging accordingly. By analyzing engagement metrics—such as likes, shares, comments, and view counts—religious leaders can determine which aspects of the narrative resonate most with their followers. This data-driven approach allows leaders to refine their messaging, ensuring that it remains relevant, impactful, and emotionally resonant. The use of data analytics ensures that the enemy narrative is not static but evolves to address the changing concerns and fears of the audience.

Using technology to amplify the idea of an enemy involves leveraging digital platforms to create a pervasive sense of threat that keeps followers engaged and united. Through social media, targeted advertising, messaging apps, content creation, visual storytelling, memes, online communities, and data analytics, religious leaders can ensure that their message reaches a wide audience and that the perceived threat remains at the forefront of their followers' consciousness. By making the enemy narrative omnipresent in the digital environment, leaders can maintain a sense of urgency and loyalty among their followers, ensuring that they remain committed to the cause and resistant to outside influences.

Chapter 8: Crafting the Enemy: A Practical Guide for Religious Leaders

The process of maintaining influence and unity within a religious community often requires the creation of a compelling adversary—someone or something that embodies the challenges and dangers faced by the faithful. By identifying and targeting ideologies that are seen as threats to the core beliefs of the faith, religious leaders can rally their followers, instill loyalty, and reinforce the boundaries between the in-group and outsiders. This chapter provides a practical guide for religious leaders on how to craft an adversary that resonates with the concerns of their community and how to use propaganda effectively to sustain followers' loyalty.

Creating a compelling adversary involves more than simply identifying an ideology that opposes the faith; it requires crafting a narrative that portrays this ideology as a direct and immediate threat. The adversary must be framed in a way that connects with the fears and anxieties of the followers—whether those fears involve threats to their moral values, the stability of their community, or their spiritual well-being. By emphasizing the harmful effects of the adversary's ideology and presenting it as something that must be resisted to preserve the faith, the leader creates a powerful and unifying narrative.

To ensure that this adversary remains a compelling focal point for the community, religious leaders must also use propaganda techniques to sustain followers' loyalty. Propaganda is most effective when it is emotional, repetitive, and reinforces existing beliefs. By repeatedly highlighting the dangers posed by the adversary and using emotive language that evokes fear, anger, or disgust, leaders can ensure that the narrative remains at the forefront of their followers' consciousness. The use of slogans, symbols, and evocative imagery can further reinforce the message, making it memorable and ensuring that it resonates on a deeper emotional level.

Sustaining followers' loyalty also requires a sense of ongoing crisis—a belief that the threat posed by the adversary is constant and requires vigilance. By framing the adversary as ever-present and emphasizing the need for unity and action, leaders can keep followers engaged and committed to the cause. The use of testimonials, personal stories, and anecdotal evidence can help make the threat feel real and immediate, further solidifying the enemy narrative and motivating followers to remain loyal to the community and its leaders.

This chapter will offer practical strategies for religious leaders looking to create a compelling adversary and sustain followers' loyalty through propaganda. It will cover techniques for targeting ideologies, crafting narratives that evoke strong emotions, and maintaining a sense of urgency within the community. By following these guidelines, religious leaders can effectively use the concept of an adversary to build unity, maintain influence, and ensure the continued loyalty of their followers in the face of both internal and external challenges.

Crafting a Persuasive Adversary: Strategies for Targeting Ideologies

IN RELIGIOUS LEADERSHIP, creating a compelling adversary is a powerful way to unify followers and strengthen commitment to the faith. By targeting ideologies that oppose or threaten the core beliefs of the community, religious leaders can craft an enemy that embodies everything they oppose. This process involves strategic framing, selective storytelling, and emotional manipulation to create a narrative that resonates deeply with followers, making the adversary appear as a real and immediate threat. Below are strategies for effectively targeting ideologies and crafting a compelling adversary.

Identify a Contradictory Ideology

The first step in creating a compelling adversary is identifying an ideology that stands in stark contrast to the community's core values. This could be secularism, materialism, atheism, or a competing religious movement. The chosen ideology must be framed as not just different but inherently harmful to the faith and community. For example, secularism can be portrayed as eroding traditional values, while materialism might be depicted as undermining spirituality. The key is to ensure that the targeted ideology is positioned as incompatible with the teachings and values of the community, setting the stage for framing it as an adversary.

Define the Adversary's Agenda

To make the adversary more tangible, it is essential to define their perceived agenda. Religious leaders should articulate what the adversary aims to achieve and how their goals threaten the community. For instance, an adversary could be depicted as seeking to weaken the faith, corrupt the morals of the younger generation, or divide the community. By defining the adversary's agenda in this way, leaders create a clear and understandable threat that followers can rally against. The narrative must present the adversary's actions as intentional and malicious, giving followers a reason to remain vigilant and united.

Use Fear-Driven Language to Highlight the Threat

Framing the adversary requires the use of language that evokes fear and urgency. Words like "corrupting," "destructive," and "dangerous" should be used to describe the ideology and its potential impact. The goal is to create a sense of fear that compels followers to take action against the ideology. By emphasizing the dangers posed by the adversary—such as the potential loss of moral values, the breakdown of community unity, or divine punishment—leaders can create a strong emotional response in their followers. This fear-driven narrative encourages the community to view the adversary as a threat that must be opposed for the sake of their spiritual survival.

Personalize the Adversary with Real-Life Examples

To make the threat of the adversary more tangible, it is effective to provide real-life examples of individuals or groups who have embraced the targeted ideology and suffered as a result. Personal stories of people who have "lost their way" or experienced negative consequences due to following the ideology help make the threat feel real and relatable. These examples serve as cautionary tales, showing followers what could happen if they allow the adversary's influence to take hold. The more personal and emotional the stories, the more they will resonate with the audience, reinforcing the sense of danger.

Create a Clear "Us vs. Them" Dynamic

To strengthen group identity and unity, it is important to create a clear distinction between the followers of the faith and the adversaries who represent the opposing ideology. The "us vs. them" dynamic fosters solidarity among followers by emphasizing their shared values and contrasting them with the perceived immorality or corruption of the adversary. This dynamic makes it easier for followers to see themselves as part of a righteous group that must stand firm against the forces of evil. By emphasizing the differences between the community and the adversary, leaders can create a sense of pride and loyalty that binds followers together.

Simplify Complex Ideas

Ideologies are often complex, and followers may struggle to understand the nuances of what they are being asked to oppose. To create a compelling adversary, it is crucial to simplify the ideology being targeted, reducing it to its most negative and threatening elements. For instance, secularism could be simplified as "a rejection of God's authority," while atheism could be framed as "a denial of all moral responsibility." By reducing complex ideas to simple, emotionally charged statements, leaders can make it easier for followers to grasp the threat and rally against it.

Associate the Adversary with Broader Social Problems

An effective way to amplify the perceived threat of the adversary is to associate them with broader social problems that followers are already concerned about. For example, an adversary promoting a progressive ideology could be linked to rising crime rates, family breakdown, or the erosion of cultural traditions. By drawing these associations, leaders create a narrative in which the adversary is not just a threat to the faith but also to the stability and well-being of society as a whole. This broader framing increases the stakes, making it more urgent for followers to resist the adversary and its influence.

Use Visual and Symbolic Imagery

Visual and symbolic imagery can be powerful tools for reinforcing the idea of an adversary. Leaders can use symbols, such as flags, logos, or specific colors, to represent the targeted ideology and create a visual reminder of the threat. Imagery that contrasts the community's values—such as images of families, sacred symbols, or peaceful gatherings—with negative depictions of the adversary can create an emotional response that reinforces the desired narrative. The use of symbols helps to make the adversary more concrete and provides followers with a clear target for their fears and opposition.

Leverage Media and Technology

The use of media and technology is essential for amplifying the enemy narrative. Religious leaders can use social media platforms, websites, blogs, and videos to spread their message and reach a wider audience. Engaging content—such as posts, live streams, articles, and podcasts—can be used to emphasize the dangers posed by the adversary and keep followers informed about the latest "threats." The constant exposure to messages that frame the adversary as a danger ensures that followers remain vigilant and committed. By leveraging technology, leaders can create an omnipresent sense of threat that keeps the community united in resistance.

Encourage Vigilance and Resistance

To sustain the enemy narrative, followers must be encouraged to remain vigilant and take action against the adversary. Religious leaders can call on followers to resist the influence of the adversary in their own lives, whether by avoiding certain behaviors, rejecting particular media, or actively opposing those who promote the targeted ideology. Encouraging followers to engage in symbolic acts of defiance—such as signing petitions, attending protests, or publicly condemning the adversary—creates a sense of empowerment and involvement. By actively participating in the resistance, followers feel that they are part of a greater struggle to protect their community and their faith.

Creating a compelling adversary involves more than just identifying an ideology that contradicts the community's beliefs; it requires a strategic approach to framing, emotional manipulation, and continuous reinforcement. By defining the adversary's agenda, using fear-driven language, personalizing the threat, establishing a clear "us vs. them" dynamic, simplifying complex ideas, associating the adversary with broader social problems, using visual imagery, leveraging media, and encouraging resistance, religious leaders can effectively target ideologies and create a powerful enemy narrative. This narrative not only unifies followers but also strengthens their commitment to the faith and motivates them to defend their beliefs against perceived threats.

Maintaining Devotion: Sustaining Followers' Loyalty Through Propaganda

PROPAGANDA IS A POWERFUL tool for maintaining loyalty and commitment among followers, especially in a religious context. By creating and reinforcing a specific narrative, leaders can ensure that their followers remain dedicated to the faith and the community. Sustaining loyalty requires more than a one-time message; it is an ongoing process that involves emotional engagement, repetition, selective storytelling, and an environment that discourages dissent. Below are key strategies for using propaganda to sustain followers' loyalty effectively.

Emotional Engagement

To sustain loyalty, the message must resonate on an emotional level. Propaganda that evokes strong emotions—such as fear, hope, pride, or anger—is more likely to create a lasting impact. Religious leaders often use fear to highlight the dangers of opposing ideologies, instilling a sense of urgency and the need for unity. At the same time, they evoke feelings of hope by promising followers a better future or divine favor if they remain loyal. By balancing fear and hope, leaders create a compelling narrative that motivates followers to stay committed. Emotional engagement is key to ensuring that followers are not only intellectually convinced but also deeply connected to the message.

Repetition of Key Messages

Repetition is one of the most effective tools in propaganda. To sustain loyalty, the core messages must be repeated consistently across different platforms and contexts. Religious leaders should use sermons, religious texts, social media, community gatherings, and written publications to reiterate the key narratives. The repetition of slogans, catchphrases, and emotionally charged statements ensures that these messages become ingrained in the minds of followers. Over time, repeated exposure to the same messages creates familiarity, and familiarity breeds acceptance. By consistently reinforcing the desired beliefs and behaviors, leaders make it difficult for followers to question or deviate from the narrative.

Selective Storytelling

Propaganda is most effective when it is rooted in stories that resonate with the audience. Selective storytelling involves choosing specific anecdotes, testimonies, or historical events that align with the desired narrative while ignoring those that contradict it. Religious leaders can use stories of past struggles and victories to inspire followers, portraying their community as part of an ongoing battle between good and evil. Personal testimonies of individuals who have benefited from their faith can also serve to validate the message and demonstrate the rewards of loyalty. By presenting only the stories that support the narrative, leaders create a consistent and compelling picture that reinforces the importance of staying committed.

Creating a Sense of Belonging
Loyalty is closely tied to the feeling of belonging. Propaganda should emphasize the importance of being part of the community and the rewards that come with it. Religious leaders can use messages that celebrate the uniqueness of their community, highlighting the values, traditions, and shared experiences that set them apart. By portraying the community as a family, followers are made to feel that their identity is closely tied to their membership. This sense of belonging is further reinforced by emphasizing the dangers of leaving the community—such as social isolation, spiritual loss, or divine punishment. By creating a strong sense of belonging, leaders can make it difficult for followers to even consider leaving.

Demonizing the "Other"
To sustain loyalty, it is important to create a clear distinction between the in-group (the faithful followers) and the out-group (those who oppose or threaten the faith). By demonizing the "other," leaders can create a sense of fear and hostility that unites followers in opposition to a common enemy. The out-group is often portrayed as morally corrupt, spiritually lost, or dangerous, making it easier for followers to justify their loyalty to the in-group. This "us vs. them" dynamic reinforces group identity and encourages followers to view their loyalty as a form of resistance against external threats. The more

followers feel that their community is under attack, the more committed they will be to defending it.

Control of Information

Controlling the flow of information is crucial for maintaining loyalty. Religious leaders can use propaganda to control what followers see, hear, and read, ensuring that they are exposed only to messages that align with the desired narrative. This can be achieved by discouraging followers from engaging with outside sources of information, labeling them as dangerous or misleading. By creating an environment where dissenting views are suppressed, leaders prevent followers from questioning the narrative or exploring alternative perspectives. This control of information ensures that followers remain focused on the messages provided by the leadership, reinforcing their loyalty and commitment.

Symbolism and Rituals

Symbols and rituals are powerful tools for sustaining loyalty. Religious symbols—such as crosses, flags, or sacred texts—serve as constant reminders of the community's values and beliefs. Rituals, whether they are daily prayers, weekly gatherings, or annual ceremonies, create a sense of continuity and reinforce the emotional bond between followers and the community. By incorporating propaganda into these rituals—such as including messages about the enemy, the rewards of loyalty, or the importance of unity—leaders can ensure that the desired narrative is consistently reinforced. The repetition of rituals creates a sense of stability and security, making followers more likely to remain loyal.

Positive Reinforcement and Rewards

Sustaining loyalty is not only about using fear and negative consequences; it also involves rewarding loyal behavior. Positive reinforcement can come in the form of public recognition, special privileges, or promises of spiritual rewards. Religious leaders can use propaganda to highlight the benefits of loyalty, such as divine favor, community support, or a sense of purpose. By celebrating examples of loyal followers and showing how they have benefited from their faith, leaders create a positive association between loyalty and personal well-being. This positive reinforcement encourages followers to remain committed and motivates others to emulate their behavior.

Emphasizing the Importance of Vigilance

To keep followers loyal, it is important to create a sense of ongoing threat that requires constant vigilance. Propaganda should emphasize that the community is always under threat from external forces—whether they are ideological enemies, cultural changes, or moral decay. By presenting loyalty as an ongoing struggle, leaders create a sense of purpose and urgency that keeps followers engaged. The narrative of vigilance ensures that followers remain alert and ready to defend their faith, making loyalty an active, rather than passive, commitment. The need for vigilance keeps followers focused on the community's goals and prevents complacency.

Using Technology to Amplify the Message

Modern technology offers powerful tools for sustaining loyalty through propaganda. Social media platforms, messaging apps, blogs, and videos can be used to reach followers directly and consistently. Leaders can create content—such as posts, videos, articles, and live streams—that reinforces the desired narrative and keeps followers engaged. By using technology to amplify the message, leaders can ensure that followers are exposed to the propaganda on a daily basis, making it an integral part of their lives. The more followers interact with this content, the more they internalize the message, strengthening their loyalty to the community.

By employing these strategies—emotional engagement, repetition, selective storytelling, fostering belonging, demonizing the "other," controlling information, utilizing symbolism and rituals, providing positive reinforcement, emphasizing vigilance, and leveraging technology—religious leaders can effectively use propaganda to sustain followers' loyalty. The goal is to create a compelling narrative that resonates emotionally, reinforces group identity, and keeps followers committed to the cause. Through continuous reinforcement, emotional connection, and control of the information environment, leaders can ensure that followers remain devoted to the faith and resistant to external influences.

Part 3: Dividing to Conquer: Social Division and the Power of Group Dynamics

Throughout history, leaders have effectively used social division as a means of creating unity within their own groups. By framing the world in terms of "us versus them," leaders can forge a powerful group identity, creating a sense of belonging and solidarity among followers. This sense of identity becomes even stronger when contrasted against an adversary—someone or something perceived as a threat. The dynamics of in-group versus out-group create an environment where loyalty, unity, and obedience are enhanced, as followers are united against a common enemy.

Social division is not only a tool for creating group identity but also for mobilizing support, energizing followers, and sustaining movements. Social movements, activists, and even online communities have all leveraged the power of opposition to solidify their identity and mobilize their base. By identifying an enemy—whether it is an ideology, a social group, or an institution—movements are able to channel anger, fear, and dissatisfaction into action. The creation of an adversary allows for a sense of purpose, a reason to fight, and a clear target for action.

Modern technology, particularly social media, has amplified the impact of social division and group dynamics. The digital age allows leaders to create echo chambers, where followers are only exposed to information that aligns with their existing beliefs. This environment strengthens the "us versus them" mentality, making it difficult for followers to see outside perspectives or question the group's narrative. Social media also provides a platform for misinformation and propaganda, allowing for the rapid spread of messages that fuel division, amplify fear, and solidify loyalty.

This part of the book will explore how leaders create and leverage social division and group dynamics to build unity and power. It will examine the psychological benefits of defining an enemy, the techniques used by social movements to solidify identity, and the role of social media in amplifying propaganda and creating echo chambers. It will also provide practical guidance for group leaders on identifying the right target group to demonize and crafting a sustainable narrative for maintaining group cohesion. By understanding these dynamics, one can gain insight into the power of division as a tool for control, mobilization, and loyalty-building.

Chapter 9: The Power of Division: Creating Group Identity Through "Us vs. Them"

The distinction between "us" and "them" is one of the most powerful ways to create a cohesive group identity. Throughout history, leaders have used the dynamics of in-groups and out-groups to foster unity, loyalty, and a sense of belonging among their followers. By defining who belongs to the group and who does not, leaders can strengthen the bonds between members and create a shared sense of purpose. This process often involves highlighting the differences between the in-group and the out-group, portraying outsiders as threats or enemies that must be resisted.

The psychological benefits of defining an enemy are profound. When individuals are given a clear adversary, they experience a heightened sense of purpose and solidarity. The presence of an enemy provides a common focus, a reason to stand together, and a way to channel frustrations and fears. This dynamic creates an emotional bond between group members, as they unite against a perceived threat. The feeling of belonging to a group that is under attack fosters loyalty and makes individuals more willing to defend their group, even at great personal cost.

In-group and out-group dynamics are not limited to political or religious contexts; they are present in all aspects of society, from sports teams to social clubs. The need to belong is a fundamental human drive, and defining an enemy provides a powerful means of satisfying that need. This chapter will explore how leaders use the concept of "us vs.

them" to create strong group identities, examining the psychological mechanisms behind in-group and out-group dynamics and the benefits of defining an enemy. Understanding these dynamics sheds light on the ways in which social division can be used to unite, control, and motivate groups.

The Dynamics of Belonging: Understanding In-Group and Out-Group Relationships

IN-GROUP AND OUT-GROUP dynamics play a critical role in shaping how individuals identify themselves, relate to others, and perceive threats. By defining who belongs to the group (the in-group) and who does not (the out-group), leaders can create a clear distinction that fosters loyalty, solidarity, and a strong sense of identity among followers. This differentiation is often at the heart of social cohesion, especially in religious, political, or social movements, where unity is essential for achieving collective goals.

In-group dynamics are characterized by a strong sense of belonging, mutual support, and shared identity. Members of an in-group perceive themselves as part of a collective with common values, beliefs, and goals. This creates an environment where members feel a deep emotional connection to the group and a sense of pride in their identity. The bond between members is reinforced through rituals, symbols, and shared experiences, which help to create a distinct identity that sets the group apart from others. The more exclusive the group feels, the stronger the sense of belonging becomes, making members more willing to defend the group against perceived threats.

Out-group dynamics, on the other hand, involve viewing those outside the group as fundamentally different, often inferior, or even dangerous. Out-groups are perceived as a threat to the in-group's values, resources, or way of life, which leads to suspicion, distrust, and sometimes hostility. This perception of the out-group as a threat can be manipulated by leaders to strengthen in-group loyalty and unity. By portraying the out-group as an enemy, leaders create a sense of urgency that compels members to band together in defense of their shared beliefs and interests. The "us versus them" mentality makes the in-group's identity clearer and more defined, as members rally together against a common adversary.

The **psychological impact** of in-group and out-group dynamics is profound. Belonging to an in-group satisfies fundamental human needs for connection, security, and identity. People derive a sense of self-worth from being part of a group that is perceived as superior or morally righteous, and this sense of superiority can be further enhanced by viewing out-groups in a negative light. The presence of an out-group creates a contrast that reinforces the in-group's values and beliefs, making members feel validated in their loyalty. This dynamic also makes individuals more likely to conform to group norms, as deviating could result in being labeled an outsider—a deeply uncomfortable and isolating prospect.

Leaders use in-group and out-group dynamics to maintain control and mobilize followers. By clearly defining who is in and who is out, leaders set boundaries that make it easier to identify and target potential threats. These boundaries also help to ensure that members remain loyal and committed to the group's objectives. The fear of being seen as part of the out-group discourages dissent and encourages conformity, as members want to avoid being excluded or ostracized. This pressure to conform can be particularly powerful in tightly knit communities, where social support and identity are closely tied to group membership.

Symbols and rituals play a key role in reinforcing in-group and out-group dynamics. In-group members often share symbols—such as flags, emblems, or clothing—that serve as visual markers of their identity. These symbols not only help to create a sense of belonging but also serve as a way to differentiate the in-group from the out-group.

Rituals, whether they are religious ceremonies, political rallies, or community gatherings, provide opportunities for members to come together, reaffirm their commitment to the group, and celebrate their shared identity. By participating in these rituals, members strengthen their emotional ties to the group and reinforce the boundaries that separate them from the out-group.

The **stereotyping of out-groups** is another important aspect of in-group and out-group dynamics. By applying negative stereotypes to those outside the group, leaders can create a simplistic and emotionally charged narrative that justifies hostility and exclusion. Out-groups are often portrayed as immoral, dangerous, or inferior, making it easier for in-group members to view them as a legitimate threat. This stereotyping not only reinforces group cohesion but also makes it easier for members to justify aggressive actions against the out-group. The more threatening the out-group is perceived to be, the more united and vigilant the in-group becomes.

In-group and out-group dynamics can also lead to **dehumanization**, where the out-group is seen as less than human or lacking in moral worth. This dehumanization allows in-group members to justify discrimination, exclusion, or even violence against those who are different. When an out-group is dehumanized, the moral constraints that typically govern behavior are weakened, making it easier for individuals to act aggressively or support punitive measures against the perceived enemy. Leaders who wish to strengthen group unity often use dehumanizing language to portray the out-group as deserving of hostility or punishment.

Understanding in-group and out-group dynamics is essential for comprehending how leaders create cohesive communities, maintain control, and mobilize followers against perceived threats. By defining who belongs and who does not, leaders create a powerful sense of identity that satisfies followers' need for belonging and security. The psychological impact of these dynamics drives conformity, loyalty, and readiness to oppose the out-group, ensuring that the community remains united and committed to its goals. The interplay between in-group cohesion and out-group hostility is a fundamental aspect of human social behavior, one that has been used throughout history to build, sustain, and manipulate social groups.

The Power of Opposition: Psychological Benefits of Defining an Enemy

DEFINING AN ENEMY PROVIDES significant psychological benefits to a group, fostering unity, solidarity, and a sense of purpose among its members. Throughout history, leaders have used the concept of an adversary to galvanize support, mobilize action, and create strong group identities. By identifying an enemy, leaders tap into deep-seated psychological needs for belonging, purpose, and security, transforming these needs into powerful tools for cohesion and loyalty.

One of the most prominent psychological benefits of defining an enemy is **enhanced group identity**. When an enemy is identified, the boundaries of the group become clearer, making it easier for members to understand what distinguishes them from others. The presence of an enemy highlights the values, beliefs, and behaviors that are unique to the group, creating a distinct and recognizable identity. This strong sense of identity gives members a feeling of belonging, as they see themselves as part of a collective that is united in its struggle against a common adversary. The more clearly defined the enemy, the stronger the sense of group identity becomes.

Defining an enemy also provides a **sense of purpose**. People have an inherent need to feel that they are part of something larger than themselves, and the existence of an enemy gives the group a mission—a reason to fight, resist, or defend. This sense of purpose can be incredibly motivating, giving members a clear goal and a sense of direction. The struggle against the enemy becomes a unifying force that brings members together, encouraging them to put aside personal differences and work toward a shared objective. The sense of purpose derived from having an enemy helps to create a cohesive and motivated group that is willing to make sacrifices for the greater good.

Another psychological benefit is the **emotional bond** that forms between group members when they face a common enemy. The perception of an external threat generates fear, anger, and anxiety—emotions that are powerful motivators for collective action. When group members share these emotions, they form stronger emotional connections with one another, as they are united in their response to the threat. This emotional bond reinforces group loyalty and creates a sense of solidarity, as members feel that they are not alone in their fears and frustrations. The shared experience of opposing an enemy fosters a sense of camaraderie and trust, making the group more resilient in the face of challenges.

Defining an enemy also helps to **simplify complex issues**, providing a convenient explanation for problems that the group faces. By attributing difficulties to the actions of an external adversary, leaders can create a clear and straightforward narrative that resonates with followers. This simplification provides a sense of certainty in an uncertain world, offering followers an easily identifiable target for their frustrations. Instead of grappling with complex, multifaceted issues, members can focus their energy on opposing the enemy, which provides a sense of control and empowerment. The enemy becomes a scapegoat for the group's problems, allowing members to channel their anger and dissatisfaction into a specific and actionable direction.

Boosting self-esteem is another key psychological benefit of defining an enemy. When the enemy is portrayed as inferior, immoral, or dangerous, it enhances the group's sense of superiority and righteousness. Members derive a sense of pride from belonging to a group that is "better" than the enemy, which boosts their self-esteem and reinforces their loyalty to the group. This sense of superiority also helps to justify the group's actions, making members feel that they are on the right side of history. The more negatively the enemy is portrayed, the more positively group members view themselves, which strengthens their commitment to the group and its cause.

Defining an enemy also **discourages dissent** within the group. The presence of an external threat creates a sense of urgency that makes internal disagreements seem trivial or even dangerous. Members are less likely to question the group's leadership or challenge its decisions when they feel that unity is essential for survival. Leaders can use the existence of an enemy to suppress dissent, framing any internal criticism as a betrayal of the group's cause. This pressure to conform ensures that members remain loyal and obedient, as they fear being seen as sympathizing with the enemy or weakening the group's position.

Finally, defining an enemy provides a **sense of security**. In a world that can be unpredictable and threatening, having a clearly defined enemy provides a way to make sense of danger. It creates a narrative in which the source of threats is external and identifiable, which can be reassuring for group members. By knowing who the enemy is, members feel that they have some control over their situation—they can take action, defend themselves, and protect their community. This sense of security, even if it is based on an oversimplified or manipulated narrative, helps to alleviate fear and anxiety, making members more comfortable and committed to the group.

The psychological benefits of defining an enemy—enhanced group identity, a sense of purpose, emotional bonding, simplification of complex issues, boosted self-esteem, discouragement of dissent, and a sense of security—are powerful motivators for loyalty and cohesion. Leaders who understand these dynamics can use them to build strong, united groups that are committed to their cause and willing to act in defense of their shared beliefs. By creating a compelling enemy narrative, leaders can transform individual needs and fears into collective strength, ensuring that the group remains focused, motivated, and united in its struggle against a common adversary.

Chapter 10: Harnessing Opposition: Leveraging Social Movements for Identity and Mobilization

Social movements often rely on the creation of opposing forces to define their identity and mobilize support. By identifying a clear adversary—whether it be an institution, a policy, or an ideology—activist groups can foster a sense of unity and purpose among their members. The presence of an opposing force serves to clearly define what the movement stands against, creating a boundary between "us" and "them" that solidifies group identity. This adversarial dynamic is crucial for transforming a collection of individuals into a cohesive group with shared goals and a clear mission.

Activist groups use ideological conflict not only to create identity but also to mobilize their followers. Conflict creates urgency, and a well-defined enemy gives supporters something to fight against. By framing their cause as a battle between right and wrong, activist leaders can inspire passion and commitment, encouraging their followers to take action. Whether it is through protests, campaigns, or social media, the presence of an enemy transforms abstract goals into tangible struggles, motivating individuals to participate actively and contribute to the movement's cause.

This chapter will explore how social movements leverage opposing forces to create and solidify their identity. It will examine the techniques used by activist groups to create ideological conflict and mobilize support, including the use of adversarial framing, emotional appeals, and the amplification of differences. By understanding these dynamics, one can see how the creation of an enemy can serve as a powerful tool for building solidarity, energizing supporters, and driving social change.

Forging Identity Through Opposition: How Activist Groups Create Opposing Forces

ACTIVIST GROUPS OFTEN define themselves in opposition to an external force or ideology. By creating and highlighting an opposing force, these groups establish a clear identity that unites their members and distinguishes them from others. The creation of an adversary provides a rallying point for the group, clarifying their mission and strengthening their collective identity. This process of defining an opponent is not only about differentiating the group but also about fostering a sense of urgency, purpose, and belonging among members.

Identifying the Opposing Force

The first step in creating an opposing force is identifying an entity, ideology, or institution that represents everything the group opposes. This could be a government policy, a corporation, a social norm, or even another activist movement. The chosen adversary must symbolize a threat or obstacle to the group's goals and values. For instance, an environmental activist group might identify a large oil company as the opposing force, framing it as a symbol of environmental destruction and corporate greed. By selecting a clear and easily identifiable target, the group creates a narrative in which their mission is defined by resisting this adversary.

Framing the Opposition as a Threat

Once the opposing force is identified, the next step is framing it as a direct threat to the group's values, goals, or the well-being of the wider community. The opposition is portrayed as not just different, but as actively harmful, creating a sense of urgency that compels members to take action. For example, a social justice group might frame systemic inequality as a threat to basic human rights, emphasizing that action must be taken immediately to combat it. By framing the opposition as a threat, the group creates a narrative of struggle and resistance, motivating members to remain actively engaged in the cause.

Simplifying the Narrative

To solidify group identity, the narrative around the opposing force must be simple and easy to understand. Activist groups often distill complex social, political, or environmental issues into a clear "good versus evil" dynamic. This simplification makes it easier for members to understand what they are fighting against and to communicate their message to others. For example, rather than discussing the intricacies of climate change policy, an environmental group might simplify the narrative by framing the opposition as "big corporations destroying the planet for profit." This straightforward framing makes it easier for members to rally around the cause and reinforces their shared identity as defenders of the environment.

Creating an Emotional Connection

A key part of solidifying group identity is creating an emotional connection between members and the cause. Activist groups use emotive language, powerful visuals, and personal stories to evoke strong emotional responses—such as anger, fear, hope, or empathy—that bind members together. By highlighting the harm caused by the opposing force, the group can generate feelings of outrage and injustice, which serve as powerful motivators for collective action. Personal testimonies of those affected by the opposing force help to humanize the issue and create a sense of urgency, making members feel personally connected to the struggle.

Using Symbols and Slogans

Symbols and slogans are important tools for reinforcing group identity and defining the opposing force. Symbols—such as logos, flags, or specific colors—help to visually represent the group and create a sense of belonging. Slogans, on the other hand, condense the group's message into a memorable phrase that can be easily repeated and shared. These symbols and slogans often include references to the opposing force, framing the group's mission as a struggle against a specific adversary. For instance, a slogan like "No Justice, No Peace" not only communicates the group's demand for justice but also implicitly defines the opposition as those who deny justice. The repeated use of symbols and slogans helps to reinforce the group's identity and keep the opposing force at the forefront of members' minds.

Creating an "Us vs. Them" Dynamic

The process of defining an opposing force inherently creates an "us versus them" dynamic, which is crucial for building group identity. This dynamic fosters a sense of solidarity, as members see themselves as part of a righteous struggle against an unjust adversary. The opposing force is portrayed as fundamentally different from the group—morally, ideologically, or even existentially. By emphasizing these differences, the group creates a clear boundary between "us" (the virtuous, the just) and "them" (the corrupt, the unjust). This boundary strengthens the bonds between members and encourages loyalty, as individuals are more likely to remain committed to a group that is engaged in a struggle against a perceived enemy.

Mobilizing Action Through Opposition

The presence of an opposing force also serves to mobilize action. Activist groups use the threat posed by the opposition to motivate members to participate in protests, campaigns, or other forms of collective action. The narrative of resistance creates a sense of duty among members, making them feel that they have a personal responsibility to take action against the adversary. By organizing events and actions that directly target the opposing force—such as protests outside corporate offices or petitions against specific policies—activist groups give their members a tangible way to contribute to the cause. This active participation reinforces group identity and provides members with a sense of empowerment, as they feel they are making a real difference in the fight against their adversary.

Reinforcing Group Loyalty Through Conflict

Conflict with the opposing force helps to reinforce group loyalty. When the group faces resistance from the adversary—such as criticism, legal challenges, or counter-protests—it validates the group's mission and strengthens the resolve of its members. The perception that the opposing force is actively trying to undermine or silence the group creates a sense of injustice, which further unites members and reinforces their commitment to the cause. This dynamic creates a cycle of escalation, where each action taken by the opposing force serves to deepen the group's identity and strengthen its resolve.

Leveraging Media to Amplify the Narrative

Activist groups also leverage media coverage to amplify the narrative of opposition. By drawing attention to the actions of the opposing force, groups can frame themselves as defenders of justice, standing up against powerful adversaries. Media coverage of protests, rallies, or confrontations with the opposition serves to legitimize the group's cause and attract new supporters. The more visible the conflict with the opposing force, the more attention the group receives, which can lead to increased support and participation. The use of social media platforms also allows groups to directly communicate their narrative to a wider audience, ensuring that the message of opposition reaches as many people as possible.

By creating and defining opposing forces, activist groups establish a clear identity that unites their members and motivates action. Through identifying an adversary, framing it as a threat, simplifying the narrative, creating emotional connections, using symbols and slogans, fostering an "us versus them" dynamic, mobilizing action, reinforcing loyalty through conflict, and leveraging media, groups are able to solidify their identity and build a cohesive and motivated community. The presence of an adversary not only provides a focal point for the group's mission but also ensures that members remain committed, engaged, and ready to fight for their cause.

Mobilizing Through Division: Techniques for Using Ideological Conflict to Gain Support

Ideological conflict can be a powerful tool for mobilizing support and building a committed base of followers. By framing issues as battles between opposing ideologies, leaders can create a sense of urgency, generate emotional engagement, and inspire action. The use of ideological conflict serves to polarize the audience, clearly defining who is on the "right" side and who represents the "enemy." The following techniques are commonly used to leverage ideological conflict for mobilizing support effectively.

Framing the Conflict in Moral Terms

One of the most effective techniques for mobilizing support is framing the ideological conflict in moral terms. By presenting the issue as a battle between good and evil, right and wrong, or justice and injustice, leaders can tap into deeply held values and emotions. This moral framing makes the conflict seem more significant than a mere difference of opinion—it becomes a matter of principle that demands action. Followers are more likely to become engaged and take action when they believe they are defending something morally righteous. The stronger the moral framing, the more compelled followers feel to stand up against the perceived injustice.

Simplifying the Narrative

Complex ideological issues can be challenging for people to understand and engage with. Simplifying the narrative is an important technique for mobilizing support. Leaders reduce the conflict to its most basic elements, creating a straightforward, emotionally charged story that followers can easily grasp. For example, instead of delving into the intricacies of economic policy, a leader might frame the conflict as "protecting hardworking citizens from greedy elites." This type of simplified narrative allows followers to understand the stakes quickly and decide which side they are on, making it easier to mobilize them in support of the cause.

Emotional Appeals

Using emotional appeals is crucial for mobilizing support in an ideological conflict. Emotions such as fear, anger, hope, and empathy are powerful motivators for action. Leaders may highlight the dangers posed by the opposing ideology, creating a sense of fear and urgency that compels followers to act. They may also use anger to channel frustration against the enemy, making it easier to rally support for protests or other forms of resistance. On the other hand, appeals to hope and the promise of a better future can inspire followers to become actively involved in the movement. The combination of fear and hope creates a compelling emotional narrative that motivates people to take action.

Defining Clear Opponents

To mobilize support effectively, it is essential to define a clear opponent. People are more likely to take action when they have a specific target for their efforts. Leaders often define the opposing ideology in terms of a person, group, or institution that embodies everything they stand against. For instance, a movement advocating for social justice might target a specific government official or corporation as the embodiment of systemic injustice. By putting a face to the enemy, leaders create a tangible target for their followers' energy, making it easier to organize actions such as protests, boycotts, or petitions against the opposing force.

Creating a Sense of Crisis

Mobilizing support often requires creating a sense of crisis that demands immediate action. Leaders frame the ideological conflict as an urgent threat that requires followers to act now rather than later. This urgency can be achieved through the use of fear-driven language, such as describing the opposing ideology as "an existential threat" or "a danger to our way of life." The sense of crisis makes followers feel that they cannot afford to stay passive—action is necessary to protect what they hold dear. This urgency serves as a powerful motivator, pushing followers to participate in activities such as rallies, campaigns, or other forms of collective action.

Using "Us vs. Them" Language

The "us vs. them" dynamic is a common technique for mobilizing support in ideological conflicts. Leaders create a clear distinction between those who are on the side of righteousness and those who represent the enemy. This language fosters a sense of unity and solidarity among followers, as they see themselves as part of a group that is fighting for a just cause. It also makes it easier to dehumanize the opponent, portraying them as fundamentally different, immoral, or corrupt. By emphasizing the differences between "us" and "them," leaders can generate a sense of loyalty and commitment among followers, making them more willing to take action against the opposing side.

Leveraging Symbols and Slogans

Symbols and slogans play an important role in mobilizing support. A powerful slogan can capture the essence of the ideological conflict in just a few words, making it easy for followers to remember and repeat. Symbols, such as flags, logos, or colors, can also serve as rallying points, creating a visual representation of the movement and its values. By using symbols and slogans, leaders can create a sense of identity and belonging among followers, making them more likely to engage in collective action. These symbols and slogans also serve as a way to differentiate the group from the opposing side, reinforcing the "us vs. them" dynamic.

Organizing Public Demonstrations

Public demonstrations, such as rallies, protests, and marches, are effective tools for mobilizing support in an ideological conflict. These demonstrations serve multiple purposes: they show strength in numbers, draw attention to the cause, and create a sense of solidarity among participants. The presence of a clear opposing force makes these demonstrations more powerful, as followers feel they are taking a stand against something tangible. The emotional energy generated during public demonstrations can be a powerful motivator, inspiring participants to stay engaged and encouraging others to join the cause. Leaders use these demonstrations to showcase the ideological conflict and demonstrate the group's determination to resist the opposing side.

Utilizing Social Media to Spread the Message

Social media has become an indispensable tool for mobilizing support in ideological conflicts. Platforms such as Facebook, Twitter, Instagram, and TikTok allow leaders to spread their message quickly and reach a wide audience. Social media can be used to share content that highlights the dangers of the opposing ideology, showcases the group's actions, and calls followers to participate in upcoming events. The use of viral content—such as videos, memes, and graphics—helps to create emotional engagement and makes the message more shareable. Social media also allows for direct interaction with followers, creating a sense of community and encouraging them to take action in support of the cause.

Reinforcing Group Identity Through Conflict

Ideological conflict is a powerful way to reinforce group identity, which in turn helps to mobilize support. When followers see themselves as part of a group that is actively engaged in a struggle, they feel a stronger connection to the group and a greater sense of loyalty. Leaders emphasize the unique values and beliefs of the group, contrasting them with the perceived dangers of the opposing ideology. This sense of identity makes followers more likely to engage in collective action, as they feel they are part of something meaningful. The more clearly defined the conflict, the more motivated followers are to defend their identity and resist the opposing force.

Highlighting Successes Against the Opponent

Celebrating successes against the opposing force is an effective way to maintain momentum and keep followers motivated. Leaders should highlight victories—whether they are changes in policy, successful protests, or shifts in public opinion—as evidence that their efforts are making a difference. These successes serve as positive reinforcement, making followers feel that their actions are worthwhile and that they are contributing to real change. By showcasing progress in the ideological conflict, leaders can inspire followers to stay committed and continue their efforts, knowing that their actions are having a tangible impact.

By using these techniques—framing the conflict in moral terms, simplifying the narrative, making emotional appeals, defining clear opponents, creating a sense of crisis, using "us vs. them" language, leveraging symbols and slogans, organizing public demonstrations, utilizing social media, reinforcing group identity, and highlighting successes—leaders can effectively use ideological conflict to mobilize support. These strategies help to create a compelling narrative that inspires followers to take action, fosters a sense of unity, and ensures that the group remains engaged and motivated in the struggle against the opposing ideology.

Mobilizing Through Division: Techniques for Using Ideological Conflict to Gain Support

IDEOLOGICAL CONFLICT can be a powerful tool for mobilizing support and building a committed base of followers. By framing issues as battles between opposing ideologies, leaders can create a sense of urgency, generate emotional engagement, and inspire action. The use of ideological conflict serves to polarize the audience, clearly defining who is on the "right" side and who represents the "enemy." The following techniques are commonly used to leverage ideological conflict for mobilizing support effectively.

Framing the Conflict in Moral Terms

One of the most effective techniques for mobilizing support is framing the ideological conflict in moral terms. By presenting the issue as a battle between good and evil, right and wrong, or justice and injustice, leaders can tap into deeply held values and emotions. This moral framing makes the conflict seem more significant than a mere difference of opinion—it becomes a matter of principle that demands action. Followers are more likely to become engaged and take action when they believe they are defending something morally righteous. The stronger the moral framing, the more compelled followers feel to stand up against the perceived injustice.

Simplifying the Narrative

Complex ideological issues can be challenging for people to understand and engage with. Simplifying the narrative is an important technique for mobilizing support. Leaders reduce the conflict to its most basic elements, creating a straightforward, emotionally charged story that followers can easily grasp. For example, instead of delving into the intricacies of economic policy, a leader might frame the conflict as "protecting hardworking citizens from greedy elites." This type of simplified narrative allows followers to understand the stakes quickly and decide which side they are on, making it easier to mobilize them in support of the cause.

Emotional Appeals

Using emotional appeals is crucial for mobilizing support in an ideological conflict. Emotions such as fear, anger, hope, and empathy are powerful motivators for action. Leaders may highlight the dangers posed by the opposing ideology, creating a sense of fear and urgency that compels followers to act. They may also use anger to channel frustration against the enemy, making it easier to rally support for protests or other forms of resistance. On the other hand, appeals to hope and the promise of a better future can inspire followers to become actively involved in the movement. The combination of fear and hope creates a compelling emotional narrative that motivates people to take action.

Defining Clear Opponents

To mobilize support effectively, it is essential to define a clear opponent. People are more likely to take action when they have a specific target for their efforts. Leaders often define the opposing ideology in terms of a person, group, or institution that embodies everything they stand against. For instance, a movement advocating for social justice might target a specific government official or corporation as the embodiment of systemic injustice. By putting a face to the enemy, leaders create a tangible target for their followers' energy, making it easier to organize actions such as protests, boycotts, or petitions against the opposing force.

Creating a Sense of Crisis

Mobilizing support often requires creating a sense of crisis that demands immediate action. Leaders frame the ideological conflict as an urgent threat that requires followers to act now rather than later. This urgency can be achieved through the use of fear-driven language, such as describing the opposing ideology as "an existential threat" or "a danger to our way of life." The sense of crisis makes followers feel that they cannot afford to stay passive—action is necessary to protect what they hold dear. This urgency serves as a powerful motivator, pushing followers to participate in activities such as rallies, campaigns, or other forms of collective action.

Using "Us vs. Them" Language

The "us vs. them" dynamic is a common technique for mobilizing support in ideological conflicts. Leaders create a clear distinction between those who are on the side of righteousness and those who represent the enemy. This language fosters a sense of unity and solidarity among followers, as they see themselves as part of a group that is fighting for a just cause. It also makes it easier to dehumanize the opponent, portraying them as fundamentally different, immoral, or corrupt. By emphasizing the differences between "us" and "them," leaders can generate a sense of loyalty and commitment among followers, making them more willing to take action against the opposing side.

Leveraging Symbols and Slogans

Symbols and slogans play an important role in mobilizing support. A powerful slogan can capture the essence of the ideological conflict in just a few words, making it easy for followers to remember and repeat. Symbols, such as flags, logos, or colors, can also serve as rallying points, creating a visual representation of the movement and its values. By using symbols and slogans, leaders can create a sense of identity and belonging among followers, making them more likely to engage in collective action. These symbols and slogans also serve as a way to differentiate the group from the opposing side, reinforcing the "us vs. them" dynamic.

Organizing Public Demonstrations

Public demonstrations, such as rallies, protests, and marches, are effective tools for mobilizing support in an ideological conflict. These demonstrations serve multiple purposes: they show strength in numbers, draw attention to the cause, and create a sense of solidarity among participants. The presence of a clear opposing force makes these demonstrations more powerful, as followers feel they are taking a stand against something tangible. The emotional energy generated during public demonstrations can be a powerful motivator, inspiring participants to stay engaged and encouraging others to join the cause. Leaders use these demonstrations to showcase the ideological conflict and demonstrate the group's determination to resist the opposing side.

Utilizing Social Media to Spread the Message

Social media has become an indispensable tool for mobilizing support in ideological conflicts. Platforms such as Facebook, Twitter, Instagram, and TikTok allow leaders to spread their message quickly and reach a wide audience. Social media can be used to share content that highlights the dangers of the opposing ideology, showcases the group's actions, and calls followers to participate in upcoming events. The use of viral content—such as videos, memes, and graphics—helps to create emotional engagement and makes the message more shareable. Social media also allows for direct interaction with followers, creating a sense of community and encouraging them to take action in support of the cause.

Reinforcing Group Identity Through Conflict

Ideological conflict is a powerful way to reinforce group identity, which in turn helps to mobilize support. When followers see themselves as part of a group that is actively engaged in a struggle, they feel a stronger connection to the group and a greater sense of loyalty. Leaders emphasize the unique values and beliefs of the group, contrasting them with the perceived dangers of the opposing ideology. This sense of identity makes followers more likely to engage in collective action, as they feel they are part of something meaningful. The more clearly defined the conflict, the more motivated followers are to defend their identity and resist the opposing force.

Highlighting Successes Against the Opponent

Celebrating successes against the opposing force is an effective way to maintain momentum and keep followers motivated. Leaders should highlight victories—whether they are changes in policy, successful protests, or shifts in public opinion—as evidence that their efforts are making a difference. These successes serve as positive reinforcement, making followers feel that their actions are worthwhile and that they are contributing to real change. By showcasing progress in the ideological conflict, leaders can inspire followers to stay committed and continue their efforts, knowing that their actions are having a tangible impact.

By using these techniques—framing the conflict in moral terms, simplifying the narrative, making emotional appeals, defining clear opponents, creating a sense of crisis, using "us vs. them" language, leveraging symbols and slogans, organizing public demonstrations, utilizing social media, reinforcing group identity, and highlighting successes—leaders can effectively use ideological conflict to mobilize support. These strategies help to create a compelling narrative that inspires followers to take action, fosters a sense of unity, and ensures that the group remains engaged and motivated in the struggle against the opposing ideology.

Chapter 11: Digital Echoes: The Role of Social Media in Propaganda and Division

Social media has transformed the way people communicate, share information, and form opinions. In the context of propaganda, it has become a powerful tool for creating echo chambers and amplifying enemy narratives. Through algorithms that prioritize engaging content, social media platforms often end up reinforcing users' existing beliefs by exposing them primarily to information that aligns with their views. This creates echo chambers—insulated online communities where members are continually fed narratives that reinforce their worldview while excluding dissenting perspectives. In these environments, enemy narratives are amplified, making the perceived threat more immediate and real, and fostering unity against the defined "other."

In addition to fostering echo chambers, social media is also a fertile ground for spreading misinformation. Propaganda relies on misinformation to create confusion, heighten fears, and sow division within societies. Social media's speed, reach, and lack of rigorous fact-checking make it an ideal medium for disseminating misleading or false information about perceived enemies. The viral nature of platforms like Facebook, Twitter, and Instagram allows misinformation to spread quickly, often reaching thousands of users before any corrections can be made. By using misinformation to fuel division, propagandists can ensure that followers remain loyal, engaged, and united against the fabricated threats.

This chapter will examine the role of social media in the propagation of propaganda, focusing on the creation of echo chambers and the use of misinformation to foster division. It will explore how algorithms, viral content, and user behavior contribute to the spread of enemy narratives and how misinformation can be used to manipulate public perception and deepen societal divides. Understanding the power of social media in shaping beliefs and reinforcing loyalty is essential for recognizing the modern dynamics of propaganda and its impact on group identity and cohesion.

Amplifying the Message: Creating Echo Chambers and Strengthening Enemy Narratives

ECHO CHAMBERS ARE POWERFUL tools for reinforcing a particular narrative and ensuring that followers remain loyal and committed. In an echo chamber, individuals are only exposed to information and perspectives that align with their existing beliefs, creating an insulated environment that amplifies the group's core messages while excluding dissenting viewpoints. The creation of echo chambers is particularly effective for amplifying enemy narratives, as it allows leaders to continuously emphasize the dangers posed by a perceived adversary, heightening followers' sense of fear, urgency, and loyalty.

Establishing Echo Chambers

The first step in creating an echo chamber is to establish an environment where followers are exposed only to the group's messages. This can be achieved through control of information sources, encouraging members to engage only with approved content, and discouraging interaction with opposing views. Online spaces—such as social media groups, private forums, or messaging channels—are particularly effective for creating echo chambers, as they allow leaders to control the flow of information and curate content that reinforces the group's beliefs. By limiting exposure to outside perspectives, the group ensures that followers receive a consistent, one-sided narrative that aligns with the leadership's objectives.

Repetition and Reinforcement

Once an echo chamber is established, repetition becomes a key tool for reinforcing the desired narrative. Leaders continuously repeat key messages about the enemy, emphasizing the threat they pose and the need for unity and resistance. The repeated exposure to these messages ensures that followers internalize them, making the enemy narrative a central part of their worldview. The more often followers hear the same messages, the more likely they are to accept them as true, regardless of whether they have been fact-checked or verified. Repetition also creates a sense of familiarity, which can lead to greater acceptance and trust in the narrative being presented.

Emotional Amplification

Emotional appeals are essential for amplifying enemy narratives within echo chambers. Leaders use fear, anger, and outrage to evoke strong emotional reactions that reinforce the sense of threat posed by the enemy. For example, stories of alleged wrongdoing by the enemy, images depicting the harm they have caused, or personal testimonies of individuals affected by their actions can all be used to evoke an emotional response. These emotional appeals make the narrative more compelling and help to create a sense of urgency, motivating followers to take action against the perceived adversary. The more emotional the content, the more likely it is to resonate with followers and be shared within the echo chamber.

Selective Exposure and Confirmation Bias

Echo chambers thrive on selective exposure and confirmation bias. Followers are encouraged to seek out information that confirms their existing beliefs and to avoid content that challenges the group's narrative. This selective exposure is facilitated by algorithms on social media platforms, which prioritize content that aligns with users' past behavior and preferences. As followers engage with content that reinforces the enemy narrative, they are presented with more of the same, creating a cycle of reinforcement. Confirmation bias—the tendency to interpret new information in a way that confirms existing beliefs—further strengthens the enemy narrative, as followers are more likely to accept information that supports their views and dismiss anything that contradicts them.

Using Influencers and Authority Figures

Leaders often use influencers and authority figures within the group to amplify enemy narratives. These individuals are seen as credible and trustworthy, making their messages more persuasive. When influencers or respected figures speak out against the enemy, followers are more likely to accept and internalize the message. This technique is particularly effective in echo chambers, as it creates a sense of consensus—if multiple trusted figures are all saying the same thing, it reinforces the perception that the narrative is true. The use of authority figures helps to strengthen the enemy narrative and ensures that followers remain aligned with the group's perspective.

Leveraging Social Media Algorithms

Social media algorithms are powerful tools for amplifying enemy narratives. Platforms like Facebook, Twitter, and YouTube use algorithms to prioritize content that generates engagement, such as likes, shares, and comments. Content that evokes strong emotions—particularly fear or outrage—is more likely to generate engagement, which means it is more likely to be promoted by the algorithm. Leaders can use this to their advantage by creating content that emphasizes the threat posed by the enemy, ensuring that it reaches a wider audience. The more followers engage with this content, the more the algorithm promotes it, creating a cycle of amplification that strengthens the enemy narrative.

Excluding Dissenting Voices

To maintain the integrity of an echo chamber, it is important to exclude dissenting voices. Leaders may use a variety of tactics to discourage or silence those who challenge the group's narrative. This can include banning dissenters from online spaces, labeling opposing viewpoints as fake news or propaganda, or creating social pressure to conform. By excluding dissenting voices, leaders ensure that followers are not exposed to information that might undermine the enemy narrative. This creates a closed environment where the group's messages are accepted without question, further reinforcing the sense of threat and the need for unity against the perceived adversary.

Amplifying Misinformation

Misinformation can be a powerful tool for amplifying enemy narratives within echo chambers. By spreading false or misleading information about the enemy, leaders can create a sense of danger that may not be based on reality but is nonetheless effective in mobilizing support. Misinformation can take many forms—such as exaggerated claims about the enemy's actions, fabricated stories, or manipulated images—and is often designed to evoke an emotional response. The closed nature of an echo chamber makes it difficult for followers to verify the accuracy of the information they receive, allowing misinformation to spread unchecked and further strengthening the enemy narrative.

Creating a Sense of Community

Echo chambers also serve to create a sense of community among followers. By framing the enemy as a common threat, leaders foster a sense of solidarity and belonging among group members. Followers feel that they are part of a larger movement, united in their opposition to the enemy. This sense of community is reinforced through shared experiences, such as participating in online discussions, attending events, or engaging in collective actions. The more connected followers feel to the group, the more likely they are to accept and amplify the enemy narrative. The sense of community also makes it difficult for individuals to leave the echo chamber, as doing so would mean losing their social support network.

Encouraging Active Participation

Active participation is key to sustaining the enemy narrative within an echo chamber. Leaders encourage followers to share content, engage in discussions, and participate in actions against the enemy. This active participation serves to reinforce the narrative, as followers become personally invested in the struggle. By sharing content that emphasizes the threat posed by the enemy, followers contribute to the amplification of the narrative and help to spread it to others within the echo chamber. The more actively followers participate, the more deeply they internalize the enemy narrative, making it a central part of their identity.

Creating echo chambers and amplifying enemy narratives involves establishing a closed environment where followers are only exposed to information that aligns with the group's beliefs, using repetition, emotional appeals, selective exposure, trusted influencers, social media algorithms, and misinformation to strengthen the narrative. By excluding dissenting voices, fostering a sense of community, and encouraging active participation, leaders can ensure that the enemy narrative remains at the forefront of followers' minds. The result is a loyal, committed group that is united in its opposition to a perceived adversary, ready to take action in defense of its shared beliefs.

Dividing Through Deception: Using Misinformation to Fuel Division

MISINFORMATION IS A powerful tool for creating division and reinforcing narratives that serve the interests of a particular group or leader. By spreading false or misleading information, leaders can manipulate public perception, create fear and distrust, and strengthen the sense of "us vs. them" that keeps their followers united against a perceived enemy. The use of misinformation allows leaders to simplify complex issues, demonize opponents, and rally their base, often at the expense of truth and social cohesion.

Crafting a Compelling False Narrative

To effectively use misinformation, it is essential to create a compelling narrative that aligns with the fears and biases of the target audience. The false information must resonate emotionally with followers and provide a clear explanation for their concerns. This often involves using misinformation to paint a simplistic picture of a complex issue, framing it in terms of "good vs. evil" or "us vs. them." For example, a leader might spread misinformation that attributes economic hardship to the actions of a specific group, positioning that group as the enemy responsible for the suffering of the community. The more emotionally charged and relatable the false narrative is, the more likely followers are to accept and internalize it.

Leveraging Confirmation Bias

Confirmation bias plays a key role in the effectiveness of misinformation. People are more likely to accept information that aligns with their pre-existing beliefs and dismiss information that contradicts them. Leaders exploit this bias by crafting misinformation that reinforces the group's worldview and existing prejudices. By repeatedly presenting misinformation that supports the group's beliefs, leaders create a feedback loop that strengthens those beliefs and makes followers more resistant to alternative viewpoints. This selective reinforcement ensures that the false narrative takes root, making it difficult for followers to question or challenge it.

Creating Emotional Resonance

Misinformation is most effective when it evokes strong emotions such as fear, anger, or indignation. Emotional responses make people more likely to share and act on information without verifying its accuracy. Leaders use misinformation to create a sense of crisis, portraying the enemy as an imminent threat that must be resisted. For example, false claims about an opposing group's intentions—such as suggesting that they are planning to harm the community or undermine its values—can generate outrage and fear. The emotional resonance of the misinformation makes it more memorable and motivates followers to take action against the perceived threat, thereby deepening divisions.

Spreading Misinformation Through Social Media

Social media is an ideal platform for spreading misinformation due to its reach, speed, and lack of regulation. Leaders use social media to disseminate misinformation quickly, ensuring that it reaches a large audience before it can be fact-checked or debunked. The algorithms used by social media platforms prioritize content that generates engagement—such as likes, shares, and comments—which often includes emotionally charged misinformation. By creating and sharing sensationalized content, leaders can ensure that their false narrative goes viral, reaching a wide audience and reinforcing the group's beliefs. The closed nature of online echo chambers further amplifies the spread of misinformation, as followers are exposed only to content that aligns with their existing views.

Discrediting Opponents

Misinformation is often used to discredit opponents and undermine their credibility. By spreading false or misleading information about the enemy, leaders can create doubt and suspicion, making it difficult for opponents to gain support or defend themselves. For example, a leader might spread misinformation suggesting that the opposing group is involved in illegal or immoral activities, even if there is no evidence to support the claim. This tactic not only damages the reputation of the opposing group but also serves to rally the leader's followers, who feel justified in their opposition. The more effectively misinformation discredits the enemy, the more united and loyal the leader's followers become.

Using Misinformation to Create Division Within the Opposing Group

Misinformation can also be used to create division within the opposing group, weakening their unity and reducing their ability to effectively challenge the leader's narrative. By spreading false information that plays on existing tensions or disagreements within the opposing group, leaders can sow distrust and suspicion, causing members to turn against one another. For instance, misinformation might suggest that certain members of the opposing group are acting in bad faith or have ulterior motives. This tactic creates internal conflict, making it difficult for the opposing group to present a united front and reducing their effectiveness as a potential threat.

Reinforcing Stereotypes and Prejudices

Another way that misinformation is used to fuel division is by reinforcing stereotypes and prejudices about the enemy. Leaders spread false information that portrays the opposing group as dangerous, immoral, or fundamentally different from the in-group. By emphasizing these negative traits, leaders create a narrative that justifies hostility and exclusion. For example, misinformation might suggest that members of the opposing group are inherently violent or untrustworthy, making it easier for followers to view them as a legitimate threat. By reinforcing stereotypes and prejudices, misinformation deepens the divide between "us" and "them," making reconciliation or understanding more difficult.

Amplifying the Narrative Through Repetition

Repetition is key to making misinformation effective. By repeating the same false claims over and over again, leaders ensure that the narrative becomes familiar and accepted by followers. The more often misinformation is repeated, the more difficult it becomes for followers to distinguish it from the truth. Repetition also creates a sense of consensus—if the same message is being heard from multiple sources, it creates the impression that it must be true. This technique is particularly effective in echo chambers, where followers are only exposed to information that aligns with the group's beliefs, making the misinformation seem even more credible.

Targeting Vulnerable Audiences

Misinformation is often targeted at audiences that are more likely to accept it without question. Vulnerable audiences may include individuals who feel marginalized, disenfranchised, or fearful about their future. By crafting misinformation that speaks to their fears and concerns, leaders can create a sense of belonging and provide a simple explanation for their problems. For example, misinformation might blame a particular group for economic hardship or social instability, providing a convenient scapegoat. By targeting vulnerable audiences, leaders can build a loyal base of followers who are motivated by fear and anger, making them more likely to support the leader's agenda.

Dismissing and Distracting From Facts

Leaders who use misinformation often dismiss credible information and facts that contradict their narrative. By labeling opposing viewpoints as "fake news" or part of a conspiracy, they create an environment where followers are discouraged from seeking out or trusting alternative sources of information. This tactic makes it easier to sustain the misinformation, as followers are less likely to be exposed to evidence that challenges it. Additionally, misinformation can be used to distract from real issues or scandals, shifting the focus onto a fabricated threat and diverting attention away from the leader's own shortcomings.

Polarizing the Community

The ultimate goal of using misinformation to fuel division is to polarize the community, creating a clear divide between "us" and "them." By spreading false information that demonizes the enemy and portrays them as a threat, leaders can ensure that followers remain loyal and committed to the cause. This polarization makes it difficult for individuals to remain neutral, as they are forced to choose between supporting the in-group or siding with the enemy. The more polarized the community becomes, the easier it is for leaders to maintain control, as followers are motivated by fear and hostility rather than rational debate or understanding.

Using misinformation to fuel division involves crafting a false narrative that aligns with the group's beliefs, leveraging confirmation bias, creating emotional resonance, using social media for rapid dissemination, discrediting opponents, creating division within the opposing group, reinforcing stereotypes, amplifying the narrative through repetition, targeting vulnerable audiences, dismissing credible information, and polarizing the community. These techniques are designed to manipulate public perception, create a sense of crisis, and strengthen group loyalty, ensuring that followers remain committed to the leader's agenda while deepening divisions within society.

Chapter 12: Strategies for Sustaining Unity: A Practical Guide for Group Leaders

For leaders seeking to create and maintain a strong, cohesive group, defining an adversary can be one of the most effective strategies. Identifying the right target group to demonize and crafting a sustainable narrative are crucial components of building a sense of solidarity and loyalty among followers. By clearly defining an enemy, leaders provide their group with a focal point—someone or something that embodies the opposition to everything they stand for. This not only strengthens in-group loyalty but also channels collective fears and frustrations into a common purpose.

Selecting the right target to demonize requires careful consideration. The chosen adversary must resonate with the concerns, values, and fears of the group. A poorly chosen target might lead to resistance or disengagement, while an effective choice will evoke a strong emotional response that reinforces group unity. Once the target is identified, the narrative around them must be crafted in a way that sustains the group's cohesion over time. The narrative should be simple, emotionally charged, and adaptable, allowing it to remain relevant as circumstances change. It must create a sense of urgency, portraying the adversary as a constant threat that demands vigilance and resistance from the group.

This chapter will provide practical guidance for group leaders on how to identify the right target group to demonize and craft a sustainable narrative that fosters group cohesion. It will cover strategies for selecting effective adversaries, framing the narrative to evoke emotional engagement, and maintaining the relevance of the enemy narrative over time. By understanding these techniques, leaders can use the dynamics of social division to build loyalty, unity, and a shared sense of purpose among their followers.

Selecting the Scapegoat: Identifying the Right Target Group to Demonize

CHOOSING THE RIGHT target group to demonize is a strategic decision that can significantly influence the cohesion, loyalty, and mobilization of a community or movement. By identifying a group that can be portrayed as a threat or obstacle, leaders can create a clear enemy narrative that serves as a rallying point for their followers. The process of selecting the right target involves understanding the fears, anxieties, and prejudices of the audience, as well as crafting a narrative that resonates emotionally and justifies the group's actions. Below are key considerations and strategies for identifying the right target group to demonize.

Assessing the Audience's Fears and Anxieties

The first step in identifying a target group to demonize is to understand the fears and anxieties of the audience. People are more likely to accept an enemy narrative if it aligns with their existing concerns and emotional state. For example, if the audience is worried about economic security, targeting a group that can be portrayed as taking away jobs or resources will resonate deeply. By tapping into these fears, leaders can create a narrative that feels personal and urgent, making it easier for followers to accept the chosen group as a legitimate threat. The more closely the enemy aligns with the audience's fears, the more effective the demonization will be.

Targeting Vulnerable or Minority Groups

Vulnerable or minority groups are often targeted for demonization because they are perceived as easy scapegoats. These groups may lack the power or resources to effectively defend themselves, making them ideal targets for blame. By choosing a group that is already marginalized or viewed with suspicion by the majority, leaders can amplify existing prejudices and portray the target as an enemy without facing significant backlash. The demonization of minority groups often plays on stereotypes and negative associations, making it easier for followers to accept the narrative and justify hostility toward the target.

Creating a Clear Contrast

The chosen target group should represent a clear contrast to the in-group, emphasizing the differences between "us" and "them." This contrast can be based on factors such as ideology, religion, ethnicity, culture, or socioeconomic status. By highlighting these differences, leaders can create a narrative in which the target group is portrayed as fundamentally incompatible with the values and identity of the in-group. This "us versus them" framing strengthens group identity by defining what the group stands for in opposition to the enemy. The more pronounced the contrast, the more effective the demonization will be in uniting the in-group against a common adversary.

Positioning the Target as a Threat

To effectively demonize a group, it is essential to position them as a direct threat to the well-being, values, or security of the in-group. This can involve framing the target as dangerous, immoral, or corrupt, suggesting that their actions or beliefs pose a risk to the community. For example, a political leader might portray an immigrant group as a threat to national security or cultural identity, while a religious leader might frame an ideological opponent as a threat to the faith. By emphasizing the danger posed by the target, leaders create a sense of urgency that compels followers to take action against the perceived enemy.

Using Simplified Narratives

Complex issues often require a simplified explanation to mobilize support effectively. Leaders use simplified narratives to explain why the chosen target group is responsible for the community's problems. This involves reducing multifaceted issues—such as economic inequality or social unrest—into a straightforward cause-and-effect relationship that blames the target group. For example, a leader might claim that "immigrants are taking all the jobs," providing a simple and emotionally charged explanation for unemployment. This simplification makes it easier for followers to understand the issue and identify the target as the cause, reinforcing the enemy narrative.

Emphasizing Historical Grievances or Stereotypes

Leaders often draw on historical grievances or stereotypes when identifying a target group to demonize. By referencing past conflicts, injustices, or stereotypes, they can tap into long-standing prejudices and resentments that may already exist within the community. This historical context provides a sense of legitimacy to the demonization, as it frames the target group as having a history of causing harm or acting against the interests of the in-group. The use of stereotypes simplifies the narrative, making it easier for followers to view the target as inherently dangerous or untrustworthy. This tactic ensures that the enemy narrative resonates with followers on a cultural and historical level.

Selecting a Group That Lacks a Strong Defense

An effective target for demonization is one that lacks the ability to defend itself effectively. Groups that are politically, economically, or socially marginalized are less likely to be able to counter the narrative being spread about them. Leaders choose targets that do not have a strong platform, influential allies, or the means to present their side of the story. This ensures that the demonization goes largely unchallenged, allowing the false narrative to take root without significant opposition. The more defenseless the target, the easier it is for leaders to portray them as the enemy without facing resistance or backlash.

Highlighting Specific Incidents as Evidence

To strengthen the enemy narrative, leaders often highlight specific incidents or actions attributed to the target group as evidence of their dangerous nature. These incidents may be real, exaggerated, or entirely fabricated, but they serve to validate the claims being made about the target. By focusing on specific examples—such as a crime committed by a member of the target group or an inflammatory statement made by a representative—leaders can create a narrative that feels tangible and credible. The more vivid and emotive the examples, the more likely followers are to accept the enemy narrative and see the target group as a legitimate threat.

Amplifying the Target's Influence

To create a sense of urgency, leaders may amplify the perceived influence or power of the target group, portraying them as a significant and growing threat. This amplification can involve exaggerating the size of the group, their intentions, or their capabilities. For example, a leader might claim that a small ideological faction is part of a larger conspiracy to undermine the community, making the threat appear more imminent and dangerous. By amplifying the perceived influence of the target, leaders can create a sense of fear and urgency that motivates followers to take action against the enemy.

Linking the Target to Broader Issues

Another effective tactic is to link the target group to broader social, economic, or political issues that followers are already concerned about. By framing the target as responsible for or contributing to these issues, leaders can create a narrative that resonates with the audience's existing worries. For instance, a leader might link a minority group to rising crime rates or economic instability, providing a convenient scapegoat for complex problems. This linkage makes it easier for followers to blame the target group for their struggles, reinforcing the enemy narrative and justifying opposition or hostility.

Maintaining Flexibility in the Narrative

Finally, it is important to maintain some flexibility in the narrative surrounding the target group. As circumstances change, the narrative may need to be adjusted to remain relevant and compelling. Leaders can adapt the narrative by emphasizing different aspects of the target group's behavior or by shifting the focus to new incidents that align with the group's fears and anxieties. This flexibility ensures that the enemy narrative remains effective over time, allowing leaders to continue using the target group as a rallying point for unity and action.

Identifying the right target group to demonize involves assessing the audience's fears, targeting vulnerable or minority groups, creating a clear contrast, positioning the target as a threat, using simplified narratives, emphasizing historical grievances, selecting a defenseless group, highlighting specific incidents, amplifying the target's influence, linking the target to broader issues, and maintaining flexibility in the narrative. By carefully selecting and framing the target, leaders can create a powerful enemy narrative that unites followers, reinforces group identity, and motivates action against the perceived threat.

Building Lasting Unity: Crafting a Sustainable Narrative for Group Cohesion

CRAFTING A SUSTAINABLE narrative is essential for maintaining group cohesion over the long term. A well-constructed narrative not only unites members in the short term but also keeps them committed to the group's values, goals, and identity as time goes on. The sustainability of a narrative relies on its adaptability, emotional resonance, and ability to provide a sense of purpose and belonging. Leaders must ensure that the story they tell remains relevant, compelling, and capable of evolving to meet the changing needs and circumstances of the group.

Establishing Core Values and Identity

The foundation of a sustainable narrative lies in clearly establishing the core values and identity of the group. The narrative should articulate what the group stands for—its mission, principles, and vision for the future. These core values provide a stable anchor for the group, giving members a sense of continuity and purpose. When members understand the group's identity and what sets it apart, they are more likely to feel a sense of pride and belonging. The narrative should also emphasize the group's uniqueness and superiority, reinforcing the idea that belonging to the group is meaningful and valuable.

Creating a Sense of Purpose

A sustainable narrative must provide members with a sense of purpose—a reason to be part of the group and to contribute to its goals. This purpose should go beyond immediate objectives and speak to a larger mission that inspires members to stay committed. For example, a political movement might frame its mission as a fight for justice and equality, while a religious group might emphasize the importance of fulfilling a divine purpose. By presenting the group's goals as part of a larger struggle or journey, leaders can create a sense of purpose that resonates with members and keeps them engaged over the long term.

Incorporating Emotional Appeals

Emotional appeals are crucial for sustaining engagement and loyalty. A sustainable narrative should evoke a range of emotions—such as hope, pride, fear, and anger—that resonate with members and motivate them to act. Hope and pride can be used to inspire members and make them feel that they are part of something significant, while fear and anger can be used to create a sense of urgency and the need for vigilance. By balancing positive and negative emotions, leaders can ensure that members remain emotionally invested in the group and its mission. The narrative should also include stories of success and resilience, reinforcing the idea that the group is capable of overcoming challenges and achieving its goals.

Defining an External Threat

The presence of an external threat is a powerful element of a sustainable narrative. Defining an enemy or adversary helps to create a clear "us vs. them" dynamic, strengthening group cohesion and reinforcing the group's identity. The threat should be portrayed as ongoing and evolving, ensuring that members remain vigilant and committed to defending the group. By framing the enemy as a constant danger, leaders can create a sense of urgency that keeps members focused on the group's mission. The threat must also be adaptable, allowing the narrative to evolve as circumstances change. This adaptability ensures that the enemy remains relevant and continues to serve as a rallying point for unity.

Maintaining Flexibility and Adaptability

A sustainable narrative must be flexible enough to adapt to changing circumstances. As the group grows, faces new challenges, or achieves certain goals, the narrative should evolve to reflect these changes. Leaders should be prepared to adjust the narrative to address new threats, opportunities, or concerns that arise. This adaptability ensures that the narrative remains relevant and compelling, preventing members from losing interest or feeling disconnected. By continually updating the story to reflect the group's current reality, leaders can maintain a sense of momentum and progress, which keeps members engaged and committed.

Incorporating Rituals and Symbols

Rituals and symbols play a key role in reinforcing a sustainable narrative. Rituals—such as regular meetings, ceremonies, or celebrations—provide opportunities for members to come together, reaffirm their commitment to the group, and experience a sense of unity. These rituals help to create a shared culture and strengthen the emotional bond between members. Symbols—such as logos, flags, or specific colors—serve as visual representations of the group's identity and values, creating a sense of pride and belonging. By incorporating rituals and symbols into the narrative, leaders can ensure that the group's story is not just told but also experienced and embodied by its members.

Highlighting Group Successes and Resilience

A sustainable narrative should celebrate the group's successes and highlight its resilience in the face of challenges. By showcasing past victories and emphasizing the group's ability to overcome obstacles, leaders can create a sense of confidence and optimism among members. This positive reinforcement makes members feel that their efforts are worthwhile and that they are part of a successful and capable group. Celebrating successes also helps to build momentum, encouraging members to stay committed and continue working toward the group's goals. The narrative should portray challenges as opportunities for growth, framing setbacks as temporary obstacles that the group can overcome through unity and determination.

Creating Personal Connections

A sustainable narrative should also create personal connections between members and the group's mission. Leaders can do this by sharing stories of individual members and their contributions to the group's goals. Personal stories humanize the narrative, making it more relatable and emotionally engaging. When members see themselves reflected in the group's story, they are more likely to feel a personal stake in its success. This sense of personal connection fosters loyalty and makes members more willing to invest their time, energy, and resources in the group's mission. By highlighting the impact that individual members have on the group's success, leaders can create a sense of empowerment and agency within the community.

Addressing Internal Challenges and Conflicts

To maintain cohesion, a sustainable narrative must also address internal challenges and conflicts within the group. Leaders should be transparent about the difficulties the group faces, framing them as part of the journey toward achieving the group's goals. By acknowledging internal challenges, leaders can prevent dissatisfaction from festering and ensure that members feel heard and valued. The narrative should emphasize the importance of unity and cooperation, encouraging members to work together to overcome internal conflicts. By framing internal challenges as opportunities for growth and strengthening the group's resolve, leaders can maintain cohesion and prevent divisions from undermining the group's mission.

Providing a Vision for the Future

Finally, a sustainable narrative must provide a compelling vision for the future. This vision should outline what the group hopes to achieve and the positive impact it will have on the community or the world. By presenting a hopeful and inspiring vision, leaders can motivate members to stay committed and work toward the group's long-term goals. The vision should be ambitious yet attainable, giving members something to strive for while ensuring that progress feels achievable. By keeping the group's focus on the future, leaders can maintain momentum and ensure that members remain dedicated to the cause.

Crafting a sustainable narrative for group cohesion involves establishing core values and identity, creating a sense of purpose, incorporating emotional appeals, defining an external threat, maintaining flexibility, using rituals and symbols, highlighting successes, creating personal connections, addressing internal challenges, and providing a vision for the future. A well-crafted narrative not only unites members in the present but also keeps them committed and engaged over time, ensuring that the group remains cohesive, resilient, and focused on achieving its goals.

Part 4: Nationalism and the Art of Enemy Creation

Nationalism has long been a potent tool for unifying a country, rallying the population, and legitimizing leadership. One of the most effective ways to harness nationalist sentiment is by creating and amplifying foreign enemies—external threats that serve as a rallying point for the population. By identifying another nation or group as a danger to the country's well-being, leaders can generate a sense of patriotism and loyalty, motivating citizens to stand united against a perceived adversary. This process not only strengthens national unity but also consolidates the power of those in leadership, who present themselves as the defenders of the nation.

Throughout history, leaders have used nationalism to manufacture foreign threats, often leveraging historical grievances, cultural differences, or political rivalries to create an "us versus them" narrative. National symbols, patriotic stories, and the strategic use of propaganda play crucial roles in reinforcing these narratives, making them resonate deeply with the population. By framing other countries as existential threats, leaders can ensure that citizens remain vigilant, loyal, and committed to defending the nation against perceived dangers.

The process of enemy creation often involves tapping into the collective memory of a nation, drawing on past conflicts, rivalries, and injustices to stir up emotions. Leaders evoke a sense of historical continuity, framing the current adversary as part of a long-standing struggle, which not only reinforces national pride but also validates present fears. This manufactured threat often serves multiple purposes:

it distracts from internal issues, unifies citizens under a common cause, and legitimizes the use of extraordinary measures in the name of national security. By focusing attention on an external threat, governments can divert criticism and dissent, presenting themselves as protectors in a time of crisis.

Symbols and stories play a crucial role in maintaining this narrative. National flags, anthems, and historical accounts are often used to evoke a sense of pride and duty, motivating citizens to stand against the "enemy." Leaders use these symbols to create an emotional connection to the idea of the nation, making the defense against foreign threats feel personal and urgent. Furthermore, propaganda that amplifies international incidents—whether real, exaggerated, or entirely fabricated—can create an atmosphere of fear and hostility, ensuring that the public remains aligned with the government's goals.

In the modern world, the use of nationalist propaganda has evolved with advancements in technology. Today, social media and instant communication allow for the rapid spread of information, making it easier for leaders to create and amplify foreign threats in real time. By leveraging international incidents and selectively framing them to incite fear and hatred, governments can create a sense of danger that keeps the population under control. This manipulation of public perception ensures that citizens see themselves as part of a larger struggle for survival, one in which their leaders are the only defense against an ever-present enemy.

In this part of the book, we will explore how nationalism has been used to create foreign enemies, from historical examples to modern applications. We will examine the power of national symbols and historical narratives, the role of propaganda in amplifying international incidents, and practical strategies for national leaders seeking to use nationalism to maintain control and unity. Understanding these tactics reveals the underlying mechanisms behind nationalist propaganda and the impact of foreign enemy creation on both domestic and international relations. We will also delve into how these strategies can manipulate public opinion, distract from internal problems, and maintain a sense of cohesion that may otherwise falter without the presence of a common adversary.

Chapter 13: Enemies Across Borders: Creating Foreign Threats Through Nationalism

Nationalism is a powerful force that can bring people together under a shared identity, but it can also be used to create divisions and manufacture foreign threats. Leaders have long understood that patriotism, when harnessed correctly, can be a potent tool for generating loyalty and unity within a population. By framing foreign nations as enemies, leaders can stoke fear, rally citizens under a common cause, and create an atmosphere where dissent is equated with disloyalty. The use of patriotism in manufacturing foreign threats serves not only to unify the public but also to distract from domestic issues and consolidate the power of those in authority.

Patriotism involves a deep emotional attachment to one's country, and this attachment can easily be turned against external groups or nations. By portraying a foreign entity as a threat to national security, culture, or values, leaders can manipulate public sentiment, creating a narrative of "us versus them" that fosters unity through opposition. Historical grievances, cultural differences, or even fabricated incidents can be used to paint another nation as an existential threat, giving citizens a reason to rally behind their leaders in defense of their homeland. In such a climate, national pride and loyalty become closely linked to opposing the perceived enemy.

History is filled with examples of nationalism being used to build foreign enemies. From the propaganda of the World Wars to the ideological conflicts of the Cold War, leaders have consistently used patriotic narratives to define external threats and mobilize their populations. By examining these historical examples, it becomes clear how nationalism can be both a tool of cohesion and a weapon of division. This chapter will explore the role of patriotism in creating foreign threats and analyze historical instances where nationalism has been used to build enemies, showing how leaders use these tactics to shape public perception and maintain control.

Patriotism as a Tool: The Role of Patriotism in Manufacturing Foreign Threats

PATRIOTISM, THE LOVE and devotion to one's country, can be a powerful unifying force, but it can also be manipulated to manufacture foreign threats. By channeling patriotic feelings, leaders can create an "us versus them" narrative that frames foreign nations or groups as enemies that threaten the country's sovereignty, values, and way of life. This process not only fosters a sense of unity among citizens but also strengthens the leader's position, as they are seen as the protector of the nation's interests.

Patriotism appeals to deep emotional attachments—feelings of pride, belonging, and duty toward one's country. Leaders tap into these emotions by portraying the nation as inherently good, just, and deserving of protection, while presenting the foreign enemy as dangerous, inferior, or morally corrupt. This dichotomy makes it easy for citizens to rally behind their country, as they see themselves as defending their homeland against an external threat. By framing the threat in patriotic terms, leaders ensure that the public feels personally invested in the struggle, which not only strengthens group cohesion but also motivates citizens to support government actions, even if they involve sacrifices.

The process of manufacturing foreign threats often involves exaggerating or fabricating incidents to create the perception that the nation is under attack. For example, a diplomatic disagreement might be framed as an attack on national honor, or economic competition might be portrayed as a deliberate attempt to weaken the country. These narratives are then spread through propaganda, using symbols like the national flag or anthem to evoke emotional responses. When citizens see their national symbols being "threatened," they are more likely to react defensively, supporting whatever measures the leadership deems necessary to protect the country.

Leaders also use historical grievances and past conflicts to manufacture foreign threats. By reminding citizens of past injustices or wars, they can create a sense of continuity between historical adversaries and present ones. This historical framing makes it easier to convince the public that the foreign nation is inherently hostile and has always been a threat to the nation's well-being. By evoking past struggles, leaders can strengthen the narrative that the current enemy is part of a long-standing effort to undermine or harm the nation, further justifying aggressive policies or military actions.

Patriotism also serves as a means of suppressing dissent. When the nation is portrayed as being under threat, those who question or criticize government actions can be labeled as unpatriotic or disloyal. This tactic creates a chilling effect, as citizens may fear being ostracized or punished for voicing opposition. By equating loyalty to the government with loyalty to the country, leaders can use patriotism to silence critics and maintain control. The narrative of a foreign threat thus becomes a tool for both unifying the public and marginalizing those who do not conform.

The role of patriotism in manufacturing foreign threats is a powerful demonstration of how emotional appeals can be used to shape public perception and behavior. By framing foreign nations as enemies, invoking historical grievances, and using national symbols to evoke strong feelings, leaders can create a narrative that unites the public and strengthens their own power. This manipulation of patriotic sentiment ensures that citizens remain focused on defending the nation, rather than questioning the actions or motives of their leaders.

Lessons from History: Using Nationalism to Construct Enemies

THROUGHOUT HISTORY, nationalism has been wielded as a tool to construct foreign enemies and unite the population against a common threat. By drawing on national pride, cultural identity, and historical grievances, leaders have successfully manufactured adversaries to rally their citizens and justify political or military actions. These historical examples illustrate how the strategic use of nationalism can be used to amplify tensions, suppress dissent, and mobilize the public toward a leader's goals.

One of the most notable examples of using nationalism to build enemies is **Nazi Germany** during the 1930s and 1940s. Adolf Hitler effectively employed nationalist propaganda to frame various groups, both domestic and foreign, as enemies of the German people. The Treaty of Versailles was portrayed as a humiliation inflicted upon Germany by foreign powers, creating a narrative of national victimhood. This sense of injustice was used to foster hatred against countries like France and the United Kingdom, presenting them as responsible for Germany's economic and political struggles. At the same time, Hitler used antisemitic propaganda to depict Jewish people as internal enemies conspiring with foreign powers to undermine the nation. This combination of foreign and domestic enemies created a powerful, unifying narrative that justified aggressive expansionist policies and ultimately led to World War II.

Another historical example is the use of nationalism by the **United States during the Cold War**. The U.S. government portrayed the Soviet Union as an existential threat to American values and freedom, framing the ideological conflict between capitalism and communism as a struggle for the survival of democracy. Through patriotic rhetoric, political leaders presented the Soviet Union as an aggressive force bent on world domination, a narrative that justified significant military spending, the establishment of NATO, and the involvement in conflicts like the Korean and Vietnam Wars. The "Red Scare" and McCarthyism further fueled public fear, using nationalism to target not only foreign enemies but also alleged communist sympathizers within the country. This intense fear of communism created a climate where dissent was equated with disloyalty, allowing the government to suppress opposition and maintain control.

Imperial Japan during the early 20th century also used nationalism to construct foreign enemies, particularly in the lead-up to and during World War II. Japanese leaders emphasized the idea of Japan's divine mission to lead and liberate Asia from Western colonial powers. By framing the United States, the United Kingdom, and other Western nations as imperial oppressors, Japan portrayed itself as a champion of Asian unity and resistance against Western dominance. This nationalist narrative was used to justify Japan's aggressive military expansion across East Asia and the Pacific, positioning the Japanese Empire as both the liberator and rightful ruler of the region. The sense of national pride and the perceived righteousness of Japan's mission united the population in support of the war effort.

The **Balkan Wars of the 1990s** provide another example of nationalism being used to build enemies. During the breakup of Yugoslavia, nationalist leaders in Croatia, Serbia, and Bosnia and Herzegovina used ethnic nationalism to create deep divisions between different ethnic groups. Political leaders like Slobodan Milošević in Serbia and Franjo Tuđman in Croatia used propaganda to portray neighboring ethnicities as enemies, emphasizing historical grievances and past conflicts to stoke fear and hatred. This nationalist rhetoric played a significant role in the outbreak of violence, leading to ethnic cleansing, atrocities, and widespread conflict. By framing other ethnic groups as existential threats, nationalist leaders were able to rally their populations in support of war and territorial expansion.

The **Falklands War** of 1982 between Argentina and the United Kingdom is another instance where nationalism was used to construct a foreign enemy. The Argentine military junta, facing domestic unrest and economic difficulties, sought to bolster national unity by focusing on the disputed Falkland Islands (known as Islas Malvinas in Argentina). By portraying the British as foreign occupiers of Argentine territory, the junta was able to generate a surge of patriotic fervor and distract the public from internal problems. This nationalist narrative led to the invasion of the Falkland Islands and the subsequent war with the United Kingdom. The British government, in turn, used nationalism to rally public support for retaking the islands, framing the conflict as a defense of British sovereignty.

These historical examples demonstrate how nationalism can be used to construct enemies, unite the population, and justify aggressive actions. By emphasizing historical grievances, cultural differences, and existential threats, leaders can create powerful narratives that resonate with their citizens, inspiring loyalty and a willingness to sacrifice for the perceived greater good. The manipulation of nationalism to build enemies is a strategy that has been employed across different cultures and eras, often with devastating consequences. Understanding these historical precedents helps shed light on how the same tactics continue to be used in the modern world to shape public perception and achieve political objectives.

Chapter 14: Rallying Through Symbols: The Power of National Symbols and Stories

Symbols and stories have always been central to creating a sense of national identity, and they play an equally powerful role in shaping how people perceive foreign nations. Leaders use national symbols—such as flags, anthems, and monuments—to evoke feelings of pride, loyalty, and unity. These symbols are not just reminders of a shared identity; they are tools that can be used to frame other countries as threats to that identity. By tapping into the deep emotions connected to these symbols, leaders can inspire citizens to stand against perceived adversaries.

Historical narratives further strengthen this emotional connection, as they provide a story of the nation's past struggles, triumphs, and adversities. These stories often highlight moments of conflict with other nations, portraying the nation as a righteous force that has faced external threats throughout its history. By emphasizing these narratives, leaders can create a sense of continuity between past and present, suggesting that the same enemies who threatened the nation before are still a danger today. This framing gives citizens a sense of purpose, as they feel they are part of an ongoing struggle to defend their homeland.

To make another country appear as an existential threat, leaders often combine the power of symbols with selective storytelling. They may evoke past conflicts, highlight cultural differences, or present exaggerated or fabricated threats to the nation's security. These tactics work together to create a narrative in which the foreign nation is seen as an ever-present danger that must be opposed. This chapter will explore how national symbols and historical narratives are used to rally citizens against others and how leaders frame other countries as existential threats to create unity and maintain control.

Symbols of Strength: Using National Symbols and Historical Narratives to Rally Against Others

NATIONAL SYMBOLS AND historical narratives are powerful tools for rallying people around a shared cause, especially when the goal is to unite them against a perceived enemy. Symbols like flags, anthems, monuments, and historical accounts evoke strong emotions, providing a visual and emotional representation of the nation's identity, struggles, and victories. Leaders use these symbols and narratives to strengthen group cohesion and create a sense of collective pride, positioning the nation as a force for good that must be defended against external threats. This emotional connection between citizens and their national identity makes it easier to mobilize the population against foreign adversaries.

National symbols serve as potent reminders of a country's heritage, culture, and values. Flags, for example, are often used to evoke patriotism and a sense of duty, especially during times of conflict. Leaders may display the national flag prominently, organize public events that include flag-raising ceremonies, or encourage citizens to wear or display the flag as a show of solidarity. The flag becomes a symbol of the nation's honor, and any perceived threat against it is portrayed as an attack on the entire country. This symbolic representation of national pride is used to create an emotional response, making citizens feel personally connected to the cause and more willing to oppose those who threaten it.

National anthems and songs are also used to rally people against others by evoking a sense of unity and collective strength. During times of tension or conflict, national anthems are played more frequently, often at public events or gatherings, to remind citizens of their shared heritage and the sacrifices made by those who came before them. The lyrics of these anthems, which often speak of bravery, sacrifice, and the defense of the homeland, serve as a call to action, inspiring citizens to stand together against foreign adversaries. By repeatedly playing these anthems, leaders reinforce the idea that the nation is under threat and that it is the duty of every citizen to protect it.

Monuments and memorials dedicated to historical events, such as wars or battles, are another tool used to rally citizens against perceived enemies. These physical symbols serve as reminders of past conflicts, often framing them as struggles for freedom or survival against foreign aggressors. Leaders use these monuments to create a sense of historical continuity, suggesting that the same enemies who threatened the nation in the past are still a danger today. By evoking the memory of past sacrifices, leaders can inspire citizens to continue the struggle and remain vigilant against external threats. Visiting these monuments, especially during national holidays or anniversaries, becomes a ritual that reinforces the narrative of defending the nation against its enemies.

Historical narratives play a critical role in shaping how citizens perceive foreign nations and their own place in the world. Leaders often emphasize specific events in history—such as wars, invasions, or colonial struggles—to create a narrative of victimhood or heroism. These stories portray the nation as having been wronged or attacked by foreign powers, creating a sense of historical grievance that can be used to justify present-day hostility. For example, leaders might evoke the memory of past wars to suggest that a neighboring country has always been an enemy and that vigilance is necessary to prevent history from repeating itself. By framing current tensions in the context of past conflicts, leaders create a narrative that feels familiar and emotionally compelling, making it easier to rally citizens against the perceived enemy.

The glorification of historical heroes is another way to use national narratives to rally against others. Leaders often invoke the memory of past leaders, soldiers, or revolutionaries who fought against foreign adversaries, presenting them as role models for the present generation. These historical figures are portrayed as embodiments of the nation's values—brave, selfless, and willing to sacrifice everything for the homeland. By glorifying these heroes, leaders create a standard of behavior that citizens are encouraged to emulate, especially during times of conflict. The message is clear: just as past generations stood up against foreign threats, so too must the current generation be prepared to defend the nation.

Educational systems are also used to reinforce national symbols and historical narratives that foster a sense of opposition to foreign threats. School curricula may emphasize certain historical events, presenting them in a way that highlights the nation's struggles against external enemies. Textbooks and lessons often frame the nation as a victim of foreign aggression or as a righteous force fighting against injustice. By instilling these narratives in young people, leaders ensure that the next generation grows up with a strong sense of national identity and a readiness to oppose those who are portrayed as adversaries. This education serves to create a shared understanding of history that aligns with the leadership's goals, making it easier to mobilize the population when needed.

Media and popular culture further amplify national symbols and historical narratives. Leaders use state-controlled or sympathetic media outlets to promote patriotic stories, broadcast historical documentaries, and highlight the importance of national symbols. Movies, television shows, and literature may also be used to depict historical conflicts, portraying the nation as a heroic force fighting against foreign aggressors. By embedding these narratives in popular culture, leaders ensure that the message reaches a wide audience, creating a sense of pride and solidarity that extends beyond official channels. The more pervasive these narratives become, the more deeply they are ingrained in the public consciousness, making it easier to rally citizens against perceived enemies.

The use of national symbols and historical narratives to rally against others is a powerful way for leaders to create unity, foster loyalty, and mobilize the population in times of conflict. By evoking emotions like pride, loyalty, and a sense of duty, leaders can create a narrative in which the nation is under constant threat from foreign adversaries, and it is the responsibility of every citizen to defend it. These symbols and stories provide a sense of continuity, linking past struggles to present challenges and ensuring that the public remains united in their opposition to perceived threats. Through the strategic use of symbols and narratives, leaders can effectively shape public perception, maintain control, and direct national sentiment against external enemies.

The Art of Fear: Framing Another Country as an Existential Threat

FRAMING ANOTHER COUNTRY as an existential threat is a powerful strategy used by leaders to rally their population, consolidate power, and justify aggressive policies or actions. By presenting a foreign nation as a direct danger to the country's survival, culture, or values, leaders can create a narrative of urgency and fear that motivates citizens to unite in defense of the homeland. This framing relies on emotional manipulation, selective use of information, and consistent messaging to shape public perception. Below are key strategies for framing another country as an existential threat.

Emphasize Differences and Incompatibilities

The first step in framing another country as an existential threat is to emphasize the fundamental differences between the two nations. Leaders focus on cultural, religious, ideological, or political distinctions to create a clear divide between "us" and "them." By portraying the foreign nation as having values or beliefs that are incompatible with those of the home country, leaders can create a sense of alienation and distrust. For example, a country with different religious beliefs might be depicted as immoral or dangerous, while a nation with an opposing political ideology might be portrayed as a threat to freedom or security. The more starkly these differences are highlighted, the easier it is to create a narrative that the foreign country poses a danger to the nation's way of life.

Use Emotional Appeals to Generate Fear

Fear is one of the most effective emotions for mobilizing a population, and leaders use it extensively when framing another country as an existential threat. They employ emotionally charged language to describe the foreign nation, using words like "dangerous," "aggressive," or "hostile" to evoke fear and anxiety. Leaders may also highlight specific incidents—whether real, exaggerated, or fabricated—that suggest the foreign nation poses a direct threat. For example, a border skirmish might be portrayed as the first step in a planned invasion, or an economic policy might be framed as a deliberate attempt to undermine the nation's economy. The goal is to create a sense of imminent danger, convincing citizens that their survival is at risk and that they must take action to defend themselves.

Highlight Past Grievances and Conflicts

Historical grievances and past conflicts are often invoked to frame another country as an ongoing threat. Leaders remind the public of previous wars, invasions, or injustices committed by the foreign nation, creating a narrative in which the current threat is part of a larger historical pattern. By emphasizing these past grievances, leaders can tap into deep-seated resentments and fears, making the foreign country seem inherently aggressive or untrustworthy. This historical framing suggests that the foreign nation has always been an enemy and will continue to be a danger unless actively opposed. The narrative of a long-standing struggle creates a sense of continuity, making it easier for citizens to accept the idea that they are once again facing an existential threat.

Portray the Foreign Country as Expansionist or Aggressive

Leaders often frame the foreign country as expansionist or aggressive, suggesting that it has ambitions that threaten the sovereignty or territorial integrity of the home nation. This portrayal may involve highlighting military actions, such as troop movements, weapons tests, or alliances, and presenting them as evidence of the foreign nation's hostile intentions. Even routine military exercises can be depicted as preparations for an invasion. By presenting the foreign country as having expansionist ambitions, leaders create a narrative in which the nation's independence and sovereignty are at risk, making it imperative for citizens to support defensive measures.

Create a Sense of Urgency

To effectively frame another country as an existential threat, it is important to create a sense of urgency. Leaders emphasize that the threat is immediate and requires a swift response. They may use phrases like "time is running out" or "we must act now" to convey the idea that inaction will lead to disaster. This sense of urgency serves to mobilize the population, convincing them that extraordinary measures—such as increased military spending, restrictions on civil liberties, or even preemptive action—are necessary to protect the nation. The urgency also makes it difficult for citizens to question or oppose the narrative, as dissent can be portrayed as weakening the country's defense at a critical moment.

Demonize the Leadership of the Foreign Country

Another effective strategy is to demonize the leadership of the foreign country, portraying them as irrational, dangerous, or malevolent. Leaders may be depicted as tyrants, extremists, or aggressors who are intent on causing harm. By focusing on the perceived flaws or ambitions of the foreign leadership, the narrative shifts from a disagreement between nations to a battle against an evil force. This framing makes it easier to dehumanize the enemy, reducing sympathy for the foreign population and justifying harsh measures. The foreign leadership is often blamed for any negative actions, which creates a clear villain in the narrative and helps to solidify the perception of the foreign nation as a threat.

Control and Manipulate Information

Controlling the flow of information is crucial for framing another country as an existential threat. Leaders use propaganda to ensure that the public is only exposed to information that supports the desired narrative, while dissenting voices are silenced or discredited. State-controlled media or sympathetic outlets are used to amplify the threat, broadcasting stories that emphasize the foreign nation's aggressive actions and hostile intentions. At the same time, leaders may dismiss or suppress information that contradicts the narrative, labeling it as fake news or enemy propaganda. By controlling what information is available, leaders can shape public perception and ensure that the narrative of an existential threat is widely accepted.

Use National Symbols to Evoke Patriotism

National symbols, such as flags, anthems, and monuments, are used to evoke feelings of patriotism and loyalty. Leaders emphasize these symbols when framing the foreign country as a threat, creating an emotional connection between the citizens and the idea of defending the nation. For example, speeches may be delivered in front of national monuments, or patriotic songs may be played during news reports about the foreign threat. By associating the defense of the nation with these powerful symbols, leaders can make the threat feel more personal and motivate citizens to rally behind the government's actions.

Isolate the Nation from Outside Influence

To strengthen the narrative of an existential threat, leaders may attempt to isolate the nation from outside influence. They portray foreign alliances, international organizations, or even foreign media as being aligned with the enemy, suggesting that any outside influence is a threat to national security. This isolationist rhetoric serves to limit the flow of information, making it more difficult for citizens to access alternative perspectives or question the narrative. It also reinforces the idea that the nation must rely on itself to defend against the threat, creating a sense of unity and self-reliance that further strengthens the leadership's position.

Depict the Threat as an Attack on Values

Finally, framing another country as an existential threat often involves depicting the threat as an attack on the nation's core values—such as freedom, democracy, or cultural identity. Leaders suggest that the foreign country not only poses a physical danger but also threatens the very essence of what the nation stands for. For example, a democratic country may frame an authoritarian regime as a threat to freedom and human rights, while a culturally homogeneous nation may depict a more diverse country as a threat to its cultural purity. By framing the threat in terms of values, leaders create a narrative that resonates on a deeper level, motivating citizens to defend not just their lives but also their way of life.

The art of framing another country as an existential threat involves emphasizing differences, generating fear, invoking historical grievances, portraying the foreign nation as aggressive, creating a sense of urgency, demonizing its leadership, controlling information, using national symbols, promoting isolation, and depicting the threat as an attack on core values. These strategies work together to create a compelling and emotionally charged narrative that unites the population, strengthens loyalty to the leadership, and justifies aggressive policies or actions. The power of this narrative lies in its ability to shape public perception, making citizens believe that their survival depends on opposing the foreign threat.

Chapter 15: Modern Manipulation: Nationalist Propaganda in Today's World

In the modern era, the use of nationalist propaganda has evolved, aided by advancements in technology and the instantaneous reach of digital media. Today, leaders can leverage international incidents—whether they are minor disputes or significant conflicts—to create narratives that incite fear and hatred. By strategically framing these events, they can turn routine diplomatic disagreements into perceived existential threats, mobilizing the public against foreign enemies and reinforcing national unity. The speed and reach of information, combined with selective framing, allow leaders to shape public opinion almost instantly, making it easier than ever to manipulate nationalist sentiment.

Modern propaganda takes advantage of the emotional power of fear and anger. International incidents—such as border disputes, economic sanctions, or accusations of espionage—are used to stoke these emotions and create a narrative in which the nation is under constant threat from hostile foreign powers. This narrative reinforces the idea that the country's survival depends on standing united against the perceived enemy, and that the leadership is the only barrier protecting the population from external dangers. The more intense the fear and hatred toward the foreign entity, the stronger the sense of loyalty and obedience to the national leadership becomes.

This chapter will explore how nationalist propaganda is applied in the modern world, focusing on how international incidents are leveraged to create fear and division. It will also examine case studies of contemporary conflicts where leaders have effectively used propaganda to craft foreign enemies, demonstrating how these tactics continue to be employed to control populations and maintain power. By understanding these modern applications, it becomes evident how deeply propaganda can influence public perception and the way people view both their nation and the rest of the world.

Exploiting Crises: Leveraging International Incidents to Create Fear and Hatred

INTERNATIONAL INCIDENTS provide fertile ground for leaders to create and amplify fear and hatred toward foreign nations. By leveraging these events—whether they are diplomatic disputes, military confrontations, economic sanctions, or perceived slights—leaders can manipulate public perception, portraying the foreign nation as a direct threat to national security, sovereignty, or values. This exploitation of international incidents is a strategic tool for rallying citizens, consolidating power, and diverting attention from domestic issues. Below are key strategies for leveraging international incidents to create a sense of fear and hatred among the populace.

Magnifying the Threat

When an international incident occurs, leaders often magnify the threat to create a sense of fear and urgency. A minor diplomatic disagreement or border skirmish can be framed as the beginning of a larger conspiracy or an aggressive action that poses an existential threat to the nation. Leaders use emotionally charged language to emphasize the gravity of the incident, suggesting that the foreign nation is intentionally seeking to provoke a conflict or undermine the country's security. By exaggerating the significance of the incident, they create an atmosphere of fear, making citizens believe that their safety and way of life are under immediate threat.

Framing the Incident as an Attack on National Honor

International incidents are often framed as attacks on national honor, pride, or sovereignty. Leaders portray the foreign nation's actions as an insult or challenge to the country's standing in the world, evoking a sense of collective outrage. This framing taps into patriotic emotions, making citizens feel personally affected by the perceived affront. For example, economic sanctions might be framed as an attempt to humiliate the nation, or a diplomatic snub might be depicted as a disrespectful attack on the country's dignity. By framing the incident as an attack on national honor, leaders can mobilize the population to rally against the foreign enemy, fostering a sense of unity and loyalty.

Using Media to Amplify the Narrative

State-controlled or sympathetic media play a crucial role in amplifying international incidents to create fear and hatred. Leaders use these media outlets to present a one-sided narrative that emphasizes the foreign nation's aggression or hostility while omitting context that might soften the perception of the event. News reports, editorials, and commentary are used to reinforce the idea that the foreign nation poses a significant threat, with frequent coverage of the incident to keep it at the forefront of the public's mind. Sensationalized reporting, including dramatic visuals and emotional language, helps to create a climate of fear and ensure that the public perceives the incident as a serious and ongoing danger.

Highlighting Vulnerability

Another key strategy is to highlight the nation's vulnerability in the face of the foreign threat. Leaders emphasize how the foreign nation's actions have exposed weaknesses or endangered the population, creating a sense of insecurity. This tactic not only instills fear but also makes citizens more receptive to government measures that are presented as necessary to protect them. For example, a cyberattack attributed to a foreign nation might be portrayed as evidence of the country's vulnerability to digital warfare, justifying increased surveillance or military spending. By emphasizing vulnerability, leaders can convince citizens that extraordinary measures are required to defend against the foreign threat, ensuring public support for their actions.

Demonizing the Foreign Nation

International incidents provide an opportunity to demonize the foreign nation, portraying it as aggressive, untrustworthy, or morally corrupt. Leaders use the incident as evidence that the foreign nation cannot be reasoned with and that it poses a danger not only to the home country but also to global stability. This demonization serves to dehumanize the foreign population, making it easier for citizens to view them as enemies and justify hostility toward them. By portraying the foreign nation as inherently evil or aggressive, leaders create a narrative in which opposition to the foreign nation is not only justified but also morally necessary.

Evoking Historical Parallels

Leaders often evoke historical parallels to strengthen the narrative of fear and hatred surrounding an international incident. By comparing the current event to a past conflict or aggression, they create a sense of historical continuity, suggesting that the foreign nation has always been a threat and will continue to be so. For example, a border dispute might be framed as part of a long history of territorial aggression by the foreign nation. By drawing on historical grievances, leaders can create a deeper emotional connection to the incident, making citizens feel that they are part of an ongoing struggle against a long-standing enemy.

Creating an "Us vs. Them" Dynamic

International incidents are leveraged to create a clear "us versus them" dynamic, emphasizing the differences between the home nation and the foreign adversary. Leaders use the incident to highlight the foreign nation's perceived flaws—whether they are ideological, cultural, or moral—and contrast them with the virtues of the home nation. This framing creates a sense of superiority and justifies hostility toward the foreign nation. By defining the foreign nation as fundamentally different and dangerous, leaders reinforce group cohesion and motivate citizens to unite against the perceived enemy.

Mobilizing Public Support for Government Actions

Once fear and hatred have been instilled, leaders use the international incident to mobilize public support for government actions. These actions may include increased military spending, diplomatic retaliation, or restrictions on civil liberties—all presented as necessary measures to protect the nation from the foreign threat. By framing these actions as a direct response to the incident, leaders can ensure that the public sees them as justified and even patriotic. The fear generated by the incident makes citizens more willing to accept sacrifices, as they believe that these measures are essential for their safety and the survival of the nation.

Isolating the Foreign Nation

Leaders may also use the international incident to isolate the foreign nation diplomatically, portraying it as a rogue state that poses a danger to the entire international community. By seeking alliances and building coalitions against the foreign nation, leaders create the perception that the home country is part of a larger effort to combat a global threat. This diplomatic isolation not only strengthens the narrative of the foreign nation's hostility but also legitimizes the government's actions in the eyes of the public. The more isolated the foreign nation appears, the more justified citizens feel in opposing it.

Exploiting Public Emotions to Sustain Fear

Finally, leaders exploit public emotions to sustain the fear and hatred generated by the international incident. They use speeches, public events, and media coverage to keep the incident fresh in the public's mind, ensuring that the fear does not dissipate. Leaders may also highlight the possibility of future incidents, suggesting that the foreign nation remains a threat and that vigilance is required. By sustaining fear and hatred, leaders can maintain public support for their policies and ensure that the population remains united against the foreign adversary.

Leveraging international incidents to create fear and hatred involves magnifying the threat, framing the incident as an attack on national honor, using media to amplify the narrative, highlighting vulnerability, demonizing the foreign nation, evoking historical parallels, creating an "us versus them" dynamic, mobilizing public support, isolating the foreign nation, and sustaining public emotions. These strategies work together to shape public perception, create a climate of fear, and rally citizens against a perceived enemy. By manipulating international incidents in this way, leaders can maintain control, divert attention from domestic issues, and strengthen their position by presenting themselves as defenders of the nation.

Modern Conflict Narratives: Case Studies of Enemy Creation

CONTEMPORARY CONFLICTS provide striking examples of how leaders and governments use propaganda and media to create and amplify the image of an enemy. In the modern world, where information is transmitted instantaneously and social media shapes public perception, the ability to construct an adversary has become even more potent. Leaders use contemporary events to instill fear, rally support, and justify their actions, often with devastating consequences for international relations. Below are several case studies that illustrate how enemy creation is used as a tactic in modern conflicts.

Russia and the West: Reviving Cold War Narratives

In recent years, Russia has leveraged narratives reminiscent of the Cold War to frame Western countries, particularly the United States and NATO, as existential threats. Russian state media and political leaders have consistently portrayed NATO's expansion and Western influence as deliberate attempts to weaken and encircle Russia. This narrative has been used to justify aggressive actions, such as the annexation of Crimea in 2014 and military interventions in Ukraine. By framing these actions as defensive moves to protect Russian sovereignty against Western encroachment, the Russian government has successfully rallied domestic support and fostered a sense of unity against a common enemy.

The United States and other Western countries, in turn, have often portrayed Russia as a major threat to global stability and democracy. Reports of cyberattacks, election interference, and military aggression are highlighted in Western media to create a narrative of Russia as a hostile actor bent on undermining democratic institutions. This portrayal has led to increased sanctions, military build-ups in Eastern Europe, and public fear of Russian influence. Both sides have used this reciprocal enemy creation to justify increased military spending and aggressive foreign policies, creating a cycle of tension that echoes the dynamics of the Cold War.

China and the United States: The New Cold War

The relationship between China and the United States has increasingly been framed as a new Cold War, with each country portraying the other as a major threat to its national interests. In China, state-controlled media frequently depict the United States as a declining power seeking to contain China's rise. This narrative is used to foster nationalism and justify China's assertive foreign policy, including territorial claims in the South China Sea and its Belt and Road Initiative. By presenting the U.S. as an aggressor trying to undermine China's economic and political development, the Chinese government has been able to generate public support for its actions and consolidate political power at home.

Conversely, in the United States, China is often portrayed as a strategic competitor and a threat to American economic and technological dominance. Political leaders have emphasized China's alleged unfair trade practices, intellectual property theft, and military expansion as threats to U.S. national security. The framing of China as an existential threat has been used to justify trade tariffs, increased military presence in the Asia-Pacific region, and legislation aimed at limiting Chinese influence. By positioning China as a rival, the U.S. government has been able to rally public support for a more confrontational approach to foreign policy.

India and Pakistan: Perpetual Rivalry and Nationalist Narratives

The long-standing rivalry between India and Pakistan offers another contemporary example of enemy creation. Both countries have used nationalist narratives to portray the other as a constant threat, particularly in relation to the disputed region of Kashmir. In India, the government has used incidents such as terrorist attacks attributed to Pakistan-based groups to create a narrative in which Pakistan is portrayed as a rogue state sponsoring terrorism. This framing has been used to justify military actions, such as airstrikes across the border, and to rally domestic support by evoking national pride and the need to protect Indian sovereignty.

Similarly, in Pakistan, India is frequently depicted as an aggressor intent on undermining Pakistan's security and sovereignty. Pakistani leaders have used this narrative to justify military spending and to maintain public support for the country's stance on Kashmir. Both sides have used incidents along the Line of Control (LoC) in Kashmir to amplify fear and hatred, portraying the other as an ever-present danger. This reciprocal enemy creation has perpetuated tensions and fueled nationalist sentiments, making diplomatic resolutions difficult to achieve.

The Middle East: Iran and Saudi Arabia's Proxy Conflicts

The rivalry between Iran and Saudi Arabia has led to a series of proxy conflicts across the Middle East, with both countries using propaganda to create and amplify the image of the other as a regional threat. In Saudi Arabia, Iran is often portrayed as a destabilizing force seeking to spread its influence through Shia militias and insurgent groups. This narrative has been used to justify Saudi interventions in countries like Yemen, where the Houthi rebels are depicted as Iranian proxies threatening Saudi borders. By framing its actions as necessary to counter Iranian aggression, the Saudi government has rallied domestic and regional support for its military campaigns.

On the other hand, Iran portrays Saudi Arabia as a puppet of Western powers, particularly the United States, and accuses it of supporting extremist groups to destabilize the region. Iranian leaders use this narrative to justify their own interventions in Syria, Iraq, and Yemen, presenting their actions as part of a broader struggle against imperialism and extremism. This enemy creation has deepened sectarian divides in the region and fueled ongoing conflicts, with both sides using fear and hatred of the other to justify their actions and maintain domestic support.

North Korea and the United States: The Threat of Nuclear Conflict

North Korea has long used the United States as the primary enemy in its state propaganda, portraying the U.S. as an imperialist aggressor intent on destroying the North Korean way of life. This narrative is reinforced through frequent state media broadcasts, military parades, and public speeches by North Korean leaders. By framing the United States as an existential threat, the North Korean government justifies its nuclear weapons program and strict control over the population. The constant portrayal of the U.S. as a looming danger helps to maintain public fear and loyalty, ensuring that the regime can continue to operate without significant internal dissent.

In the United States, North Korea is often depicted as a rogue state led by an irrational and dangerous regime. Media coverage frequently emphasizes North Korea's nuclear tests, missile launches, and human rights abuses, creating a narrative in which North Korea is portrayed as an unpredictable threat to global security. This portrayal has been used to justify military exercises in the region, economic sanctions, and diplomatic isolation. By framing North Korea as a major threat, U.S. leaders have been able to maintain public support for a hardline stance and ensure that the issue remains a priority in international relations.

These contemporary case studies demonstrate how leaders and governments use enemy creation as a tool to rally domestic support, justify aggressive policies, and maintain power. By leveraging international incidents, amplifying perceived threats, and using propaganda to create fear and hatred, leaders can shape public perception and mobilize their populations against foreign adversaries. These strategies not only exacerbate tensions and fuel conflicts but also serve to distract from domestic issues and consolidate political control. Understanding these modern examples of enemy creation helps to reveal the underlying motivations behind international conflicts and the role of propaganda in shaping global dynamics.

Chapter 16: The Strategic Playbook: Using Nationalism to Build Foreign Threats

National leaders have long used nationalism as a strategic tool to maintain control and unity within their countries. By crafting and amplifying a foreign threat, they can create a common enemy that serves to rally the population, foster loyalty, and suppress dissent. The process of building and promoting an external threat involves a series of deliberate steps designed to shape public perception, instill a sense of danger, and position the leadership as the nation's protector. When executed effectively, this strategy can significantly bolster the leader's power while ensuring that citizens remain focused on defending the nation rather than questioning internal issues.

Nationalism is particularly effective in fostering a sense of collective identity and solidarity. Leaders use patriotic messages, national symbols, and emotionally charged rhetoric to create a narrative that frames the nation as exceptional and under constant threat from outside forces. By presenting themselves as defenders of national values and sovereignty, leaders can strengthen their legitimacy and keep the population united in the face of perceived dangers. The narrative of a foreign threat not only diverts attention away from internal challenges but also creates an environment where dissent is discouraged, as it may be seen as weakening the nation in a time of crisis.

This chapter will provide a practical guide for national leaders on how to build and amplify a foreign threat. It will outline the steps involved in identifying and framing a foreign enemy, using propaganda to amplify the perceived danger, and leveraging nationalist sentiment to maintain control and unity. By understanding these tactics, leaders can effectively use nationalism to solidify their power, keep their citizens aligned with their agenda, and ensure that any opposition is marginalized or silenced.

Escalation Blueprint: Steps to Build and Amplify a Foreign Threat

BUILDING AND AMPLIFYING a foreign threat involves a strategic series of steps designed to shape public perception, foster national unity, and consolidate power. By portraying another nation as a danger to the country's security or values, leaders can generate fear, justify aggressive policies, and suppress dissent. The process requires a careful blend of propaganda, emotional manipulation, and control over the narrative. Below are the steps involved in creating and amplifying a foreign threat.

Identify and Select the Target Nation

The first step is to identify a foreign nation that can be effectively framed as a threat. This target is usually chosen based on pre-existing tensions, cultural differences, or historical conflicts that can be exploited. The selected nation should be one that has a history of disagreements or rivalry with the home country, making it easier to build on existing biases or resentments. Additionally, the target should be perceived as having the capability to pose a threat, whether it be military, economic, or ideological, to ensure that the narrative resonates with the public.

Highlight and Magnify Incidents

Once the target nation is chosen, the next step is to highlight any incidents involving that country that can be framed as aggressive or hostile. These incidents can range from border skirmishes and diplomatic disputes to economic sanctions or cyberattacks. Even minor or routine events can be magnified to create the impression that the foreign nation is acting provocatively. Leaders use media coverage and official statements to draw attention to these incidents, portraying them as deliberate acts of aggression that threaten the home nation's security.

Frame the Incident as Part of a Larger Threat

After an incident is highlighted, it is important to frame it as part of a larger, ongoing threat. Leaders emphasize that the foreign nation's actions are not isolated but are part of a broader agenda to undermine or harm the country. This framing creates a sense of continuity and suggests that the target nation has hostile intentions that require a strong response. By linking the current incident to past actions or disputes, leaders can create a narrative in which the foreign nation has always been a threat, thereby strengthening the perception of danger.

Invoke Nationalism and Patriotism

Nationalism and patriotism are powerful tools for rallying the population against a foreign threat. Leaders use patriotic language and national symbols, such as flags and anthems, to evoke a sense of pride and duty. By presenting the foreign threat as an attack on the nation's sovereignty or values, leaders can inspire citizens to rally behind the government in defense of the homeland. This invocation of patriotism helps to create an "us versus them" mentality, uniting the population against the perceived enemy and fostering a sense of loyalty to the leadership.

Demonize the Foreign Nation and Its Leadership

To amplify the threat, it is important to demonize the foreign nation and its leadership. Leaders use propaganda to portray the target nation as morally corrupt, aggressive, or dangerous. The foreign leadership is often depicted as irrational or malevolent, making it easier to dehumanize the enemy and justify hostile actions. By focusing on the perceived flaws of the foreign leadership, the narrative shifts from a diplomatic disagreement to a struggle against an evil force, thereby deepening public fear and hatred.

Control the Narrative Through Media

Controlling the narrative is crucial for building and amplifying a foreign threat. Leaders use state-controlled or sympathetic media to ensure that the public is exposed only to information that supports the desired narrative. News reports and commentary are used to emphasize the threat posed by the foreign nation, while dissenting voices are suppressed or discredited. Sensationalized coverage, dramatic visuals, and emotional language help to keep the threat at the forefront of the public's mind, ensuring that the perception of danger remains strong.

Create a Sense of Urgency

To mobilize the population, it is essential to create a sense of urgency. Leaders emphasize that the foreign threat is immediate and requires a swift and decisive response. Phrases like "we must act now" or "our future is at stake" are used to convey the idea that inaction will lead to disaster. This sense of urgency makes citizens more willing to accept aggressive measures, such as increased military spending or restrictions on civil liberties, as they believe these actions are necessary to protect the nation.

Justify Government Actions as Necessary Defense

Once the threat is established, leaders use it to justify government actions that might otherwise be controversial or unpopular. These actions can include military buildups, economic sanctions, or crackdowns on dissent. By framing these measures as necessary for defending the nation, leaders can ensure public support and minimize opposition. The fear generated by the perceived threat makes citizens more likely to accept sacrifices and less likely to question the leadership's decisions.

Suppress Dissent and Label Opponents as Traitors

To maintain control and prevent opposition, leaders use the narrative of a foreign threat to suppress dissent. Those who question the government's actions or the validity of the threat are labeled as unpatriotic or even traitors. This tactic creates a chilling effect, discouraging criticism and ensuring that the population remains unified in its support for the government's policies. By equating loyalty to the government with loyalty to the nation, leaders can marginalize opponents and maintain a tight grip on power.

Sustain the Threat Narrative Over Time

Finally, to ensure that the perception of the foreign threat remains strong, leaders must sustain the narrative over time. This involves continuously highlighting new incidents, reinforcing the idea that the threat is ongoing, and reminding the public of the foreign nation's hostile intentions. Periodic public events, such as military parades or patriotic speeches, are used to keep the population engaged and vigilant. By maintaining the narrative of an ever-present threat, leaders can ensure that the public remains loyal and supportive, even in the face of economic hardship or other domestic challenges.

Building and amplifying a foreign threat involves a series of deliberate steps: identifying the target nation, magnifying incidents, framing them as part of a larger threat, invoking nationalism, demonizing the foreign leadership, controlling the narrative, creating urgency, justifying government actions, suppressing dissent, and sustaining the narrative over time. These strategies work together to shape public perception, create a climate of fear, and rally citizens behind the leadership. By manipulating the image of a foreign threat, leaders can maintain control, justify aggressive policies, and ensure that the population remains united in defense of the nation.

Harnessing Patriotism: Using Nationalism to Maintain Control and Unity

NATIONALISM CAN BE a powerful tool for maintaining control and unity within a country, especially during times of crisis or instability. By appealing to a shared sense of national identity, leaders can rally citizens around a common cause, foster loyalty, and suppress dissent. Nationalism evokes strong emotional ties to the nation, positioning the government as the defender of the country's sovereignty, culture, and values. Below are several ways in which nationalism can be used to maintain control and unity.

Promoting a Common Identity

Nationalism emphasizes a shared national identity that transcends differences such as class, religion, or regional affiliation. Leaders use symbols like the flag, national anthem, and cultural icons to create a sense of belonging among citizens. By promoting the idea that all members of the nation are part of a larger family with a common heritage and destiny, leaders can foster unity and reduce internal divisions. This sense of collective identity makes citizens more likely to prioritize the well-being of the nation over their individual interests, strengthening social cohesion.

Framing the Nation as Under Threat

A key tactic in using nationalism to maintain control is to frame the nation as being under threat from external enemies or internal subversive elements. By creating a narrative of danger, leaders can generate fear and urgency, which motivates citizens to rally behind the government as the protector of the nation. The perception of an external threat fosters a sense of solidarity, as citizens feel they must come together to defend the country. It also creates an environment where dissent is discouraged, as questioning the government's actions may be seen as undermining the national effort to counter the threat.

Glorifying National History and Heroes

Nationalism often involves the glorification of the nation's history and the celebration of national heroes. Leaders emphasize moments of past greatness—such as victories in wars, resistance against colonial powers, or major achievements—to instill pride and a sense of national purpose. Historical figures who fought for the nation's independence or defended it against foreign adversaries are portrayed as role models, and their stories are used to inspire loyalty and sacrifice. By glorifying the nation's past, leaders can create a narrative in which the country's current struggles are part of a larger, heroic journey, thereby encouraging citizens to remain loyal and committed.

Creating an "Us vs. Them" Dynamic

Nationalism is often used to create a clear distinction between "us"—the citizens who are loyal to the nation—and "them"—those who are perceived as outsiders or enemies. This "us vs. them" dynamic helps to unite citizens by emphasizing their commonalities and distinguishing them from those who are seen as threats to the nation. Leaders may portray minorities, immigrants, or political dissidents as outsiders who do not belong, using this narrative to rally the majority and foster a sense of unity. This tactic can also be used to marginalize and discredit opposition, as those who do not conform to the nationalist narrative are labeled as traitors or enemies.

Leveraging National Symbols and Rituals

National symbols and rituals are powerful tools for fostering unity and reinforcing a sense of loyalty. Leaders organize public events such as parades, national holidays, and ceremonies that celebrate the nation's achievements and honor its heroes. These events create a sense of collective experience, allowing citizens to come together and express their pride in the nation. The repeated use of national symbols, such as the flag and anthem, helps to create an emotional connection between citizens and the country, reinforcing their loyalty and commitment. By embedding these symbols and rituals in everyday life, leaders ensure that the sense of national identity remains strong and that citizens remain united.

Promoting National Economic Interests

Nationalism can also be used to promote economic policies that are framed as being in the national interest. Leaders may encourage citizens to buy domestically produced goods, support local industries, and take pride in the nation's economic achievements. By portraying economic success as a source of national pride, leaders can rally citizens behind government initiatives and policies. This economic nationalism not only fosters a sense of unity but also allows leaders to justify protectionist policies or restrictions on foreign trade. Citizens are more likely to accept these policies if they believe they are necessary to protect the nation's economic sovereignty and ensure prosperity.

Suppressing Dissent in the Name of Unity

Nationalism can be used to suppress dissent and maintain control by equating loyalty to the government with loyalty to the nation. Leaders frame any criticism of government policies as unpatriotic, suggesting that those who oppose the government are acting against the interests of the country. This tactic creates a chilling effect, as citizens may fear being labeled as traitors or enemies of the state if they speak out. By portraying dissent as a threat to national unity, leaders can marginalize opposition and maintain a firm grip on power, ensuring that the population remains loyal and compliant.

Using Media to Reinforce Nationalist Narratives

The media plays a crucial role in promoting nationalist narratives and ensuring that the public remains aligned with the government's agenda. State-controlled or sympathetic media outlets are used to broadcast messages that emphasize the importance of national unity, celebrate the nation's achievements, and highlight external threats. The media also portrays the government as the defender of the nation, reinforcing the idea that loyalty to the government is synonymous with loyalty to the country. By controlling the narrative and ensuring that the public is exposed only to information that supports the nationalist agenda, leaders can shape public perception and maintain control.

Fostering a Sense of Collective Sacrifice

Nationalism often involves fostering a sense of collective sacrifice, where citizens are encouraged to put the interests of the nation above their own. Leaders may call on citizens to make sacrifices—such as accepting higher taxes, rationing resources, or serving in the military—in the name of national defense or progress. By framing these sacrifices as necessary for the greater good, leaders can ensure that citizens remain committed and willing to endure hardship for the sake of the nation. This sense of collective sacrifice strengthens unity, as citizens feel that they are all working together toward a common goal.

Highlighting External Achievements and International Recognition

Leaders use nationalism to maintain unity by highlighting the nation's achievements on the international stage, such as successes in sports, technological advancements, or diplomatic victories. These achievements are portrayed as evidence of the nation's greatness and are used to instill pride among citizens. By emphasizing the nation's accomplishments and its recognition by the international community, leaders create a narrative in which citizens feel that they are part of a successful and respected country. This sense of pride fosters loyalty and unity, as citizens are motivated to support the government in maintaining the nation's positive image.

Harnessing nationalism to maintain control and unity involves promoting a common identity, framing the nation as under threat, glorifying national history, creating an "us vs. them" dynamic, leveraging national symbols, promoting economic interests, suppressing dissent, using media to reinforce nationalist narratives, fostering collective sacrifice, and highlighting external achievements. These strategies work together to foster a strong sense of national identity and loyalty, ensuring that citizens remain united in their support for the government and willing to defend the nation against perceived threats. Through the careful use of nationalist sentiment, leaders can maintain control, rally the population, and suppress opposition, ensuring that the nation remains cohesive and aligned with their agenda.

Part 5: The Mechanics of Manipulation: Practical Propaganda Techniques

Propaganda is an art form that has been honed over centuries to influence public perception, manipulate emotions, and control narratives. In the modern age, with the advent of mass media, social platforms, and advanced communication technologies, the power and reach of propaganda have grown exponentially. Leaders, groups, and governments use a variety of carefully crafted techniques to shape public opinion, spread specific messages, and control how people perceive both allies and enemies. Whether it is to gain support, incite hatred, or maintain power, propaganda remains one of the most effective tools for molding the collective mindset of a society.

This part of the book delves into the practical techniques of creating and disseminating propaganda, offering a comprehensive guide to the tactics that can make or break a campaign. It begins with the fundamentals of crafting effective messaging, emphasizing the critical elements of repetition, simplicity, and emotional appeal that make propaganda so powerful. Messages that are repeated often enough tend to be accepted as truth, even without evidence. The simpler the message, the easier it is for people to grasp and internalize. Emotional appeal, particularly the use of fear, anger, or pride, helps to bypass rational scrutiny and directly engage with an audience's feelings, ensuring that the message resonates on a deeper level. Understanding how to design compelling visuals, slogans, and narratives can be the difference between a message that resonates deeply and one that is easily forgotten.

Fear and misinformation are the lifeblood of many successful propaganda campaigns, and leveraging these emotions requires skillful manipulation of facts and the creation of narratives that bypass rational scrutiny. This section explores techniques for creating fear without evidence, spreading misinformation, and managing fact-checkers who may challenge the propaganda. When fear is invoked, people are more likely to overlook inconsistencies and accept drastic actions taken by leaders. Spreading misinformation serves to create confusion, making it harder for people to discern the truth. In the age of fact-checkers, it is also important to know how to handle debunking attempts effectively, either by discrediting the fact-checkers, shifting the narrative, or overwhelming the public with so much information that the truth becomes buried.

The rise of digital platforms has transformed how propaganda is delivered, allowing messages to reach a global audience almost instantaneously. Creating viral campaigns and using digital tools like bots, trolls, and fake accounts to amplify messages have become essential components of modern propaganda strategies. Social media algorithms are designed to promote content that generates engagement, making them perfect vehicles for spreading emotionally charged propaganda. By creating content that goes viral—whether through shocking visuals, catchy slogans, or controversial statements—leaders can rapidly influence public perception and create momentum for their cause. The digital space offers endless opportunities to create and spread enemy narratives and influence the perception of millions. Automated accounts (bots), coordinated harassment from trolls, and fake profiles allow for the manipulation of conversations and the illusion of widespread support or outrage, giving the appearance that a narrative is more popular or controversial than it truly is.

Finally, no propaganda campaign is complete without addressing the inevitable resistance that arises. Understanding how to handle opposition, discredit critics, and reinforce the enemy narrative over time is crucial for maintaining control and ensuring the longevity of the propaganda effort. Leaders must know how to label dissenters as unpatriotic or align them with the enemy, creating a chilling effect that discourages others from speaking out. Techniques for managing resistance also involve redirecting blame, shifting the conversation, or drowning out opposing voices with overwhelming support from loyal followers. Moreover, reinforcing the enemy narrative requires ongoing effort—reminding the public of the threat, highlighting new incidents, and keeping the fear alive. This section will provide practical advice on countering resistance and keeping the narrative intact, ensuring that the message remains powerful and pervasive in the minds of the audience.

By understanding and applying these practical propaganda techniques, leaders can effectively shape public perception, control the flow of information, and ensure that their messages are deeply embedded in the collective consciousness. This part of the book serves as a step-by-step guide for anyone looking to master the art of propaganda, whether for political, social, or ideological purposes, showing just how powerful and dangerous effective messaging can be when used to influence masses and build or destroy public sentiment.

Chapter 17: The Foundation of Influence: Crafting Effective Messaging

The success of any propaganda campaign depends largely on the effectiveness of its messaging. Crafting a message that resonates deeply with an audience requires more than just words—it demands a strategic approach that leverages human psychology to ensure that the intended message is internalized and remembered. Repetition, simplicity, and emotional appeal are the foundational pillars of effective propaganda, each playing a critical role in shaping how a message is received and retained by the public. By mastering these elements, a message can bypass critical thinking, appeal directly to emotions, and become embedded in the collective consciousness.

Repetition reinforces the message, making it more familiar and ultimately more believable. People tend to accept information that they hear repeatedly, regardless of its accuracy, as familiarity breeds acceptance. Simplicity ensures that the message is easily understood by everyone, regardless of their education or background. The more straightforward a message, the easier it is for people to grasp, remember, and spread. Emotional appeal, meanwhile, engages the audience on a personal level, bypassing rational scrutiny and appealing directly to their fears, hopes, or pride. A message that evokes a strong emotional response is more likely to be remembered and acted upon.

In addition to crafting the words themselves, visual design is an essential component of effective messaging. The use of compelling visuals, catchy slogans, and well-crafted narratives can significantly enhance the impact of the message. Visual elements like symbols, colors, and images help to evoke emotions and create a strong association between the message and its intended meaning. Slogans distill complex ideas into short, memorable phrases that can be easily repeated, while narratives provide context, making the message feel more relatable and urgent.

This chapter will explore the key elements of crafting effective messaging, focusing on the importance of repetition, simplicity, and emotional appeal, as well as the art of designing visuals, slogans, and narratives for maximum impact. By understanding these techniques, the process of creating propaganda becomes a powerful means to shape public perception, influence behavior, and control the narrative.

The Power of Persuasion: Repetition, Simplicity, and Emotional Appeal

THE EFFECTIVENESS OF a propaganda campaign lies in its ability to resonate deeply with the audience, and this is achieved through three fundamental principles: repetition, simplicity, and emotional appeal. These elements work together to ensure that a message not only reaches the audience but also influences their thoughts and behaviors on a deep level. Mastering these techniques is crucial for crafting propaganda that sticks in the public consciousness and shapes their perception over time.

Repetition is one of the most powerful tools in propaganda. By repeating the same message over and over, it becomes familiar and ingrained in the audience's mind. People tend to believe information that they encounter frequently, as familiarity breeds a sense of truthfulness, even in the absence of evidence. This phenomenon is known as the "illusory truth effect." Repetition works to normalize the message, making it part of everyday discourse. It ensures that the intended narrative remains at the forefront of the audience's thoughts, ultimately influencing their beliefs and decisions. The more often a message is repeated, the more difficult it becomes for the audience to question it, as it becomes accepted as a common understanding.

Simplicity is equally important in effective messaging. A simple message is easy to understand, remember, and repeat. People are more likely to embrace a message if it is straightforward and accessible, rather than complex or nuanced. The goal of propaganda is not to foster critical thinking or debate but to create a narrative that is easy to accept and spread. Simple messages often use clear, direct language, avoiding ambiguity or technical jargon. This makes them more relatable and easier for people from all walks of life to grasp. Slogans, for example, are effective because they condense a complex idea into a few memorable words that can be easily repeated. Simplicity also makes it easier for the message to be spread organically, as people are more likely to share something they understand well.

Emotional appeal is the third key component of effective messaging, as emotions drive action more powerfully than logic or reason. By appealing to emotions such as fear, anger, pride, or hope, a message can bypass rational scrutiny and connect with the audience on a deeper level. Fear is particularly effective, as it triggers a survival response, making people more likely to accept drastic measures or follow authority. Anger can be used to rally people against a perceived enemy, while pride can foster loyalty to a cause or leader. Emotional appeals make the message feel personal, engaging the audience in a way that logical arguments cannot. When people feel something strongly, they are more likely to internalize the message and act upon it, whether that means supporting a leader, rejecting an opposing group, or spreading the propaganda further.

These three elements—repetition, simplicity, and emotional appeal—work synergistically to create a powerful and effective propaganda campaign. A simple message, repeated often and delivered with emotional intensity, becomes difficult for the audience to ignore or question. It shapes their perception of reality, influencing not only how they see the world but also how they react to it. Mastering these techniques allows propagandists to craft messages that stick, spread, and ultimately control the narrative in a way that rational debate and factual information often cannot achieve.

Crafting Impact: Designing Visuals, Slogans, and Narratives for Maximum Influence

VISUALS, SLOGANS, AND narratives are essential components of a propaganda campaign, serving as the vehicles that carry the message into the public consciousness. When used effectively, these elements can capture attention, evoke strong emotions, and ensure that the message is remembered and spread. The design of each component must be deliberate, ensuring that it resonates with the audience and leaves a lasting impression. By understanding how to craft powerful visuals, concise slogans, and compelling narratives, propagandists can maximize the impact of their message and influence public perception on a large scale.

Visuals are often the first point of contact with an audience, and they have an immediate emotional impact. Effective visuals use imagery that is symbolic and evocative, capable of conveying complex ideas quickly and clearly. Symbols like flags, colors, or images associated with national pride or cultural identity can evoke feelings of loyalty, fear, or anger. For example, using the national flag alongside images of a perceived enemy can create a powerful emotional response, reinforcing the idea that the enemy is a threat to the nation's sovereignty. Visuals must be designed to be striking, memorable, and easily recognizable, ensuring that they grab attention and evoke the desired emotion at a glance. Additionally, consistent use of colors and symbols helps to create a cohesive visual identity, making the campaign more effective and reinforcing the intended message every time the visuals are seen.

Slogans play a crucial role in condensing the message into a short, memorable phrase that can be easily repeated. The most effective slogans are simple, direct, and emotionally charged. They often make use of rhetorical devices such as rhyme, alliteration, or repetition to make them more memorable. Slogans are designed to be catchy and easily spread, becoming a part of everyday conversation and ensuring that the message is consistently reinforced. They should evoke an emotional response—whether that is fear, pride, or a sense of urgency—so that they resonate deeply with the audience. A well-crafted slogan can become synonymous with the cause it represents, making it a powerful tool for rallying support and creating a sense of unity among followers.

Narratives provide the context and background that give meaning to the visuals and slogans. They tell the story that the audience is meant to believe, shaping how they perceive the world around them. An effective narrative creates a clear distinction between "us" and "them," defining the enemy, the threat they pose, and the solution offered by the propagandist. Narratives must be emotionally engaging and relatable, allowing the audience to see themselves as part of the story. They often draw on existing fears, grievances, or hopes, weaving them into a story that feels personal and urgent. A well-crafted narrative is consistent and adaptable, allowing it to evolve over time as circumstances change while maintaining the core message. It provides a framework that makes the audience feel as though they are part of something larger, whether that is a fight for survival, a struggle for justice, or a mission to protect their way of life.

By carefully designing visuals, slogans, and narratives, propagandists can create a campaign that captures attention, evokes emotion, and influences behavior. The visuals draw the audience in, the slogans distill the message into something easily remembered, and the narrative provides the context that makes the message meaningful. Together, these elements ensure that the propaganda is not only seen and heard but also internalized and acted upon, creating a powerful influence over public perception and behavior.

Chapter 18: Weaponizing Uncertainty: Using Fear and Misinformation

Fear is one of the most effective tools for controlling and manipulating public perception. It overrides logic, appeals to primal instincts, and compels people to act in ways they might not otherwise consider. When fear is invoked, people become more willing to accept drastic measures, follow authority without question, and turn against perceived enemies. However, fear doesn't always need to be based on facts—it can be crafted without solid evidence and still achieve the desired effect. The power of fear lies not in its factual basis but in its ability to resonate with people's insecurities and anxieties.

Misinformation, meanwhile, serves to further the goals of fear-based propaganda by clouding the truth, creating confusion, and making it difficult for people to distinguish fact from fiction. When misinformation is skillfully spread, it undermines trust in credible sources, divides public opinion, and generates a climate of uncertainty. This uncertainty is fertile ground for fear, allowing the message to take root and grow.

This chapter explores the techniques for creating fear without evidence, such as using vague warnings, suggesting imminent danger, and presenting worst-case scenarios as likely outcomes. It also delves into the strategic use of misinformation, providing insights on how to spread false information effectively while handling fact-checkers and attempts to debunk the narrative. Fact-checkers can be a significant obstacle to the success of a propaganda campaign, but their influence can be minimized through discrediting, deflecting, or overwhelming them with a flood of information. Understanding these techniques is essential for anyone looking to master the art of fear-based propaganda and misinformation, as they reveal the true power of manipulating public sentiment and keeping an audience aligned with the intended narrative.

Instilling Fear: Techniques for Creating Fear Without Evidence

FEAR IS ONE OF THE most effective emotions for influencing people, as it bypasses rational thought and triggers primal instincts for survival. Even when there is no solid evidence to support a perceived threat, it is still possible to instill fear and manipulate public perception. By using carefully crafted techniques, propagandists can create an atmosphere of anxiety and urgency, motivating people to support drastic measures or rally against a perceived enemy. Below are key techniques for creating fear without relying on factual evidence.

Vague Warnings and Ambiguity

One of the most effective ways to create fear is to issue vague warnings that suggest an imminent threat without providing specific details or evidence. Statements like "There are threats lurking that could endanger our safety" or "We have reason to believe that danger is closer than we think" evoke fear without being tied to verifiable facts. The lack of specificity makes it difficult for critics to disprove the claim, while the ambiguity allows the audience's imagination to fill in the gaps. People tend to fear the unknown, and ambiguous warnings exploit this fear by suggesting that something bad is happening, even if there is no concrete evidence.

Use of Hypothetical Scenarios

Another technique is to present hypothetical worst-case scenarios as if they are likely outcomes. For example, saying, "If we don't act now, we could see our cities overrun by violence," paints a picture of chaos that plays on people's fears. The hypothetical nature of the statement makes it impossible to disprove, while the vivid imagery evokes an emotional response. By emphasizing what "could" happen, propagandists create a sense of urgency and anxiety that pushes people to support precautionary measures, even when there is no evidence to suggest that such scenarios are realistic.

Leveraging Anecdotal Evidence

Anecdotal evidence—isolated stories or events—can be used to create the illusion of a larger threat. By focusing on a single event and presenting it as representative of a broader trend, propagandists can create fear without the need for factual data. For example, highlighting one instance of a crime committed by a member of a particular group and suggesting that it is indicative of a larger pattern of behavior can evoke fear and distrust of that group. Anecdotes are powerful because they are relatable and evoke an emotional response, making them more persuasive than abstract statistics. By repeating these anecdotes frequently, the audience begins to perceive them as part of a larger, more threatening trend.

Appeal to Authority

Referencing unnamed authorities or experts is another way to create fear without providing evidence. Phrases like "Experts warn that the threat is real" or "Authorities are concerned about the potential dangers" lend credibility to the message without requiring specific proof. The audience is encouraged to trust the expertise of these unnamed sources, even if no concrete evidence is presented. The appeal to authority creates a sense of legitimacy, making the audience more likely to accept the warning as fact. This technique is particularly effective when the audience already has a level of trust in the leadership or institution delivering the message.

Amplification of Isolated Incidents

Amplifying isolated incidents, such as minor conflicts or isolated attacks, can create the perception of a widespread threat. By repeatedly covering these incidents in the media and using emotionally charged language, propagandists can create a sense of fear and urgency that goes beyond the actual scope of the event. For example, a single act of violence can be portrayed as part of a broader trend of instability, with terms like "rising threat" or "growing danger" used to suggest that the problem is escalating. By focusing attention on these incidents and ignoring evidence to the contrary, propagandists can create a distorted perception of reality that fosters fear.

Emotional Language and Imagery

The use of emotionally charged language and imagery is crucial for creating fear without evidence. Words like "crisis," "danger," "threat," and "catastrophe" evoke strong emotional reactions that bypass rational analysis. Visual imagery, such as pictures of destruction, terrified faces, or ominous symbols, reinforces the message and makes the fear feel more immediate. By appealing directly to emotions, propagandists ensure that the audience reacts instinctively rather than critically. The more intense the emotional response, the less likely the audience is to question the validity of the claim.

Creating a Sense of Urgency

Instilling a sense of urgency is a key element of creating fear. By emphasizing that immediate action is needed to avoid disaster, propagandists can push the audience to support measures without questioning them. Phrases like "We must act now" or "Time is running out" create pressure and make people feel that they have no choice but to comply. The sense of urgency also discourages critical thinking, as people are more focused on responding quickly than on evaluating the evidence. The more imminent the threat appears, the more likely people are to accept extreme or authoritarian measures to address it.

Association with Past Fears

Another effective technique is to link the current perceived threat to past fears or traumatic events. By drawing parallels between the present situation and previous crises—such as wars, terrorist attacks, or economic collapses—propagandists can evoke the emotions associated with those past events. This technique relies on the audience's memory of past fears to create anxiety about the present. For example, comparing a political opponent to a historical dictator or likening a current situation to a previous national disaster can create fear without needing to provide concrete evidence that the comparison is valid. The emotional resonance of past events makes the present threat feel more real and urgent.

Demonizing the "Other"
Creating fear often involves demonizing a particular group or entity, portraying them as inherently dangerous or malicious. By using dehumanizing language and portraying the target as fundamentally different from "us," propagandists can create fear without evidence. The audience is encouraged to see the targeted group as a threat simply because they are "other" or "not like us." This fear of the unknown and unfamiliar is a powerful tool, as it plays on deep-seated biases and prejudices. The less the audience knows about the targeted group, the easier it is to create a narrative that they are dangerous, without needing to provide concrete evidence to support the claim.

These techniques—vague warnings, hypothetical scenarios, anecdotal evidence, appeals to authority, amplification of isolated incidents, emotional language and imagery, creating urgency, associating with past fears, and demonizing the "other"—are all effective ways to create fear without evidence. By tapping into the audience's emotions, bypassing critical thinking, and fostering a sense of immediate danger, propagandists can manipulate public perception and motivate people to act in ways that they might not otherwise consider. Fear, once instilled, becomes a powerful force that shapes behavior, attitudes, and beliefs, making it an essential tool in the arsenal of effective propaganda.

Misinformation Tactics: Spreading Falsehoods

and Handling Fact-Checkers

MISINFORMATION IS A powerful weapon in the realm of propaganda, used to confuse, mislead, and manipulate public perception. Spreading misinformation effectively involves crafting narratives that are difficult to disprove, creating confusion, and overwhelming the audience with conflicting information. The goal is to shape public perception by planting doubts and ensuring that the truth becomes hard to discern. However, the rise of fact-checkers and independent media has created new challenges for propagandists, making it necessary to develop strategies for countering attempts to debunk misinformation. Below are techniques for spreading misinformation and handling fact-checkers to maintain control over the narrative.

Crafting Plausible Falsehoods

The first step in spreading misinformation is to ensure that the falsehoods being presented are plausible enough to be believed by the audience. Rather than fabricating completely outlandish claims, effective misinformation contains a mix of truth and lies, making it more difficult to disprove. By including some factual elements, propagandists create a veneer of credibility that makes the falsehoods seem more convincing. For example, a claim that exaggerates real data or takes statements out of context can be more persuasive than an outright fabrication. The goal is to make the false information appear credible enough that the audience is willing to accept it as truth.

Exploiting Cognitive Biases

Misinformation spreads more effectively when it taps into existing cognitive biases and preconceptions. People are more likely to believe information that aligns with their existing beliefs, a phenomenon known as confirmation bias. Propagandists use this to their advantage by crafting messages that resonate with the audience's preconceived notions, fears, or prejudices. By targeting specific groups with tailored misinformation that aligns with their beliefs, the false information is more likely to be accepted and shared. The more the misinformation reinforces what the audience already believes, the less likely they are to question it or seek out alternative viewpoints.

Flooding the Information Space

Another effective tactic for spreading misinformation is to flood the information space with numerous false or misleading claims. By overwhelming the audience with a constant stream of conflicting information, propagandists create confusion and make it difficult for people to determine what is true. This technique, often referred to as "information overload," ensures that the truth is buried beneath a mountain of falsehoods, making it harder for the audience to discern reality. When people are presented with too much information, they may become fatigued and ultimately give up on trying to find the truth, making them more susceptible to accepting the misinformation.

Creating Emotional Narratives

Misinformation is more likely to spread if it is emotionally compelling. Propagandists use emotionally charged language, sensational stories, and vivid imagery to make the false information more engaging and memorable. By appealing to emotions like fear, anger, or sympathy, the misinformation becomes more relatable and is more likely to be shared by the audience. People are more inclined to act on and spread information that evokes a strong emotional response, even if they have not verified its accuracy. By making the misinformation emotionally impactful, propagandists can ensure that it reaches a wider audience and is accepted without critical analysis.

Leveraging Social Media and Bots

Social media is a powerful tool for spreading misinformation, as it allows for rapid dissemination and amplification. Propagandists use bots, trolls, and fake accounts to spread false information across social media platforms, creating the illusion of widespread support or consensus. Automated accounts can be used to share misinformation en masse, increasing its visibility and making it appear more credible.

Trolls can engage with real users, spreading false information and sowing discord. Fake accounts, posing as ordinary individuals, lend credibility to the misinformation by making it seem like it is coming from multiple independent sources. The goal is to create a false sense of consensus, making the misinformation appear more legitimate.

Preemptively Discrediting Fact-Checkers

Fact-checkers pose a significant threat to the effectiveness of misinformation, as they work to expose falsehoods and provide accurate information. To counter this, propagandists often preemptively discredit fact-checkers by portraying them as biased, unreliable, or aligned with the enemy. By labeling fact-checkers as part of a conspiracy or accusing them of having an agenda, propagandists can undermine their credibility in the eyes of the audience. If the audience believes that fact-checkers are untrustworthy, they are less likely to accept the corrections and more likely to stick to the misinformation they have already internalized.

Shifting the Narrative

When fact-checkers attempt to debunk misinformation, propagandists may respond by shifting the narrative to avoid direct confrontation. Rather than addressing the specific points raised by fact-checkers, they redirect the conversation to a different issue, often one that evokes a strong emotional response. This tactic serves to distract the audience from the debunking attempt and refocus their attention on a new topic. For example, if a false claim about a foreign threat is debunked, the propagandist might shift the narrative to emphasize the need for national security in general, thus avoiding the specific debunking while still reinforcing the overall message.

Casting Doubt and Creating False Equivalence

Another technique for handling fact-checkers is to cast doubt on the truth by creating false equivalence between the misinformation and the debunked facts. Propagandists may say things like, "There are two sides to every story" or "The truth lies somewhere in the middle," suggesting that the misinformation is just as valid as the fact-checked information. By creating doubt and suggesting that the truth is subjective, propagandists make it harder for the audience to discern what is real. This false equivalence undermines the credibility of the fact-checkers and leaves the audience unsure of whom to trust.

Repetition of the Original Claim

Even after misinformation has been debunked, repeating the original false claim can still be effective. Repetition reinforces familiarity, and the more often a message is heard, the more likely it is to be accepted as true, regardless of whether it has been disproven. Propagandists continue to repeat false claims even after they have been debunked, knowing that some people will still accept them. This technique takes advantage of the fact that people tend to remember the initial claim more strongly than the correction, especially if the misinformation aligns with their existing beliefs.

Attacking the Messenger

A common tactic for handling fact-checkers is to attack the individuals or organizations attempting to debunk the misinformation. By launching personal attacks or questioning the motives of the fact-checkers, propagandists can shift the focus away from the content of the debunking and onto the character of those presenting it. For example, accusing a fact-checker of being politically biased or having ulterior motives serves to discredit their work and create skepticism among the audience. If the audience questions the integrity of the fact-checkers, they are more likely to dismiss the debunking and continue believing the misinformation.

Spreading misinformation and handling fact-checkers involves crafting plausible falsehoods, exploiting cognitive biases, flooding the information space, creating emotional narratives, leveraging social media, discrediting fact-checkers, shifting the narrative, casting doubt, repeating false claims, and attacking the messenger. These techniques work together to create confusion, shape public perception, and undermine attempts to expose the truth. By effectively using these tactics, propagandists can maintain control over the narrative and ensure that misinformation remains pervasive, influencing the thoughts, emotions, and behaviors of the audience.

Chapter 19: Digital Domination: Leveraging Digital Platforms for Propaganda

The rise of digital platforms has fundamentally transformed how information is shared, consumed, and manipulated. In the modern age, a message can reach millions of people within seconds, creating both opportunities and challenges for those seeking to influence public perception. Social media, in particular, has become a battleground for propaganda, offering a powerful means to spread narratives, shape opinions, and build or destroy reputations. With algorithms that prioritize engagement, emotionally charged content can spread like wildfire, making it easier than ever to influence public sentiment and craft a pervasive enemy narrative.

Creating viral campaigns is a key element of leveraging digital platforms for propaganda. By crafting content designed to provoke strong emotional responses—such as anger, fear, or outrage—leaders can ensure that their message is widely shared and reaches a broad audience. Videos, memes, and sensationalized stories are often used to make the content relatable, shareable, and memorable. The goal is not just to spread a message but to create a movement, generating momentum that makes the narrative feel inevitable and omnipresent.

Bots, trolls, and fake accounts play an essential role in amplifying these narratives and creating the illusion of widespread support or opposition. Bots can be used to flood social media platforms with posts, comments, and shares, creating a sense of popularity or urgency around a particular message. Trolls, on the other hand, engage directly with real users, spreading disinformation, sowing discord, and intimidating critics. Fake accounts add credibility by posing as genuine individuals or influencers, making it appear that ordinary people support the narrative. Together, these tools create a coordinated effort to manipulate public perception, ensuring that the message reaches its intended audience and has the desired impact.

This chapter will explore how digital platforms can be leveraged to create viral campaigns, use automated and coordinated tactics to influence perception, and ensure that the enemy narrative remains at the forefront of public consciousness. By understanding the power of digital tools and techniques, one can effectively harness the reach and immediacy of the online world to build and sustain a powerful propaganda campaign.

Going Viral: Creating Campaigns to Spread the Enemy Narrative

CREATING VIRAL CAMPAIGNS is a powerful way to spread an enemy narrative effectively and ensure that it reaches a wide audience. Viral content has the unique ability to capture attention, evoke strong emotions, and spread rapidly across digital platforms, making it a potent tool for influencing public perception. The goal of a viral campaign is to generate momentum around the enemy narrative, making it seem both inevitable and widely supported. Achieving this requires a careful blend of creativity, emotional resonance, and strategic distribution. Below are key strategies for creating viral campaigns that spread the enemy narrative.

Identify and Target Emotions

The first step in creating a viral campaign is to identify the emotions that will drive people to share the content. Fear, anger, and outrage are particularly powerful emotions that compel people to act and share messages with others. By crafting a narrative that evokes these emotions, propagandists can ensure that the audience feels a strong connection to the message. For instance, portraying the enemy as a direct threat to personal safety, family values, or cultural heritage can generate intense feelings of fear and anger, prompting people to spread the content to warn others or rally support.

Use Visually Compelling Content

Visual content is more likely to go viral than text alone. Images, videos, and graphics can communicate the enemy narrative in an impactful and memorable way, making it more likely that the audience will engage with and share it. Visuals should be designed to evoke emotion—whether through powerful imagery that depicts the threat posed by the enemy, symbols that reinforce national pride, or dramatic portrayals of potential danger. Short videos, infographics, and memes are especially effective for capturing attention and conveying the narrative quickly. The more visually compelling the content, the greater its potential to spread across social media platforms.

Craft Catchy Slogans and Hashtags

Catchy slogans and hashtags are essential for creating viral campaigns. Slogans distill the enemy narrative into a few powerful words that are easy to remember and repeat, making them ideal for spreading the message. Hashtags serve as a way to organize the conversation and make it easy for users to find and engage with related content. The key is to create slogans and hashtags that are simple, emotionally charged, and resonate with the audience. For example, a hashtag like "#DefendOurNation" can be used to evoke a sense of urgency and duty, encouraging people to join the campaign and spread the message.

Leverage Influencers and Amplifiers

To ensure that the enemy narrative reaches a wide audience, it is important to leverage influencers and amplifiers—individuals or groups with large followings who can help spread the content. Influencers, whether they are public figures, celebrities, or online personalities, have the ability to reach large numbers of people and lend credibility to the campaign. By getting influencers to share the content, propagandists can increase its visibility and make it more likely to go viral. Amplifiers can also include online communities, forums, or social media groups where the narrative is likely to resonate. By targeting these amplifiers, the campaign can reach a more engaged audience that is willing to share and promote the message.

Utilize Shock Value and Controversy

Shock value and controversy are powerful tools for capturing attention and driving engagement. Content that is shocking, provocative, or controversial is more likely to be noticed and shared, as it elicits a strong emotional response. For example, using sensational headlines, graphic images, or provocative statements can create a sense of urgency and compel people to share the content to either express their outrage or alert others. Controversy also generates discussion, which can help to spread the enemy narrative further as people engage in debates and arguments. The more polarizing the content, the more likely it is to go viral.

Create a Sense of Collective Identity

A successful viral campaign should create a sense of collective identity among the audience, making them feel that they are part of something larger. By framing the enemy narrative as a fight to protect shared values, culture, or community, propagandists can foster a sense of unity and motivate people to join the cause. Messages that include phrases like "We must stand together" or "Protect our way of life" appeal to the audience's desire for belonging and solidarity. When people feel that they are part of a collective effort, they are more likely to share the content and encourage others to do the same.

Encourage User-Generated Content

User-generated content is an effective way to amplify a viral campaign, as it encourages the audience to actively participate in spreading the narrative. By inviting people to create their own content—such as videos, memes, or personal stories—that aligns with the enemy narrative, propagandists can increase the reach of the campaign and create a sense of grassroots support. User-generated content adds authenticity and diversity to the message, making it more relatable and harder to dismiss. It also helps to keep the campaign fresh, as new content continues to be generated and shared by the audience.

Use Bots and Fake Accounts to Amplify Reach

Bots and fake accounts are essential tools for amplifying the reach of a viral campaign. Bots can be used to automate the sharing of content, ensuring that it is constantly being posted and re-posted across social media platforms. This creates the illusion of widespread interest and support, making the message appear more popular than it actually is. Fake accounts can be used to engage with real users, share personal stories, or create the impression that ordinary people are genuinely concerned about the threat posed by the enemy. By coordinating these efforts, propagandists can create a feedback loop that amplifies the enemy narrative and increases its visibility.

Monitor Engagement and Adapt

To maximize the impact of a viral campaign, it is important to monitor engagement and adapt the strategy based on what is resonating with the audience. Social media analytics can provide insights into which content is being shared the most, which messages are generating the most engagement, and which demographics are responding most strongly. By analyzing this data, propagandists can refine their messaging, create more of the content that is working, and target specific groups more effectively. A successful viral campaign is not static—it evolves in response to audience feedback, ensuring that the message remains relevant and impactful.

Exploit Timely Events and Crises

Timely events and crises provide an opportunity to launch or amplify a viral campaign. By linking the enemy narrative to current events—such as political conflicts, natural disasters, or acts of violence—propagandists can make the message feel urgent and relevant. Timely content is more likely to capture attention, as people are already focused on the event in question. By framing the event in a way that supports the enemy narrative, propagandists can capitalize on the heightened emotions and drive engagement. The key is to act quickly, ensuring that the content is released while the event is still fresh in the public's mind.

Creating viral campaigns to spread an enemy narrative involves targeting emotions, using compelling visuals, crafting catchy slogans and hashtags, leveraging influencers, utilizing shock value, creating a sense of collective identity, encouraging user-generated content, using bots to amplify reach, monitoring engagement, and exploiting timely events. By combining these strategies, propagandists can create a powerful campaign that captures attention, spreads rapidly, and shapes public perception of the enemy. The goal is to generate momentum, ensuring that the enemy narrative becomes deeply embedded in the public consciousness and difficult to challenge.

Digital Manipulation: Using Bots, Trolls, and Fake Accounts to Influence Perception

IN THE DIGITAL AGE, social media platforms have become powerful tools for shaping public opinion and influencing perception. Bots, trolls, and fake accounts are essential components of modern propaganda campaigns, used to amplify messages, create false narratives, and manipulate public discourse. By leveraging these digital tools, propagandists can create the illusion of widespread support, generate controversy, and silence dissenting voices. Below are the methods for effectively using bots, trolls, and fake accounts to influence perception and shape the narrative.

Deploying Bots for Amplification

Bots are automated accounts programmed to perform specific actions, such as liking, sharing, and commenting on posts. They are highly effective in amplifying propaganda messages, as they can operate at scale, sharing content across social media platforms 24/7. Bots can be used to increase the visibility of propaganda by generating large volumes of engagement—likes, retweets, and shares—that make the message appear popular and credible. This artificial amplification creates the illusion that the content has widespread support, encouraging real users to engage with and share it as well. Bots can also be used to manipulate trending topics, ensuring that the propaganda message appears at the top of social media feeds and attracts more attention.

Creating Echo Chambers with Bots

Another use of bots is to create echo chambers, where the same message is repeated across multiple accounts and platforms, reinforcing the intended narrative. By programming bots to post similar content across different channels, propagandists can create an environment in which users are constantly exposed to the same ideas, making them more likely to accept the message as truth. Echo chambers are particularly effective because they limit exposure to alternative viewpoints, creating a closed feedback loop that reinforces the propaganda. The more users see the same message repeated, the more they perceive it as a widely accepted truth.

Using Trolls to Disrupt and Intimidate

Trolls are individuals or automated programs that engage with real users to disrupt conversations, spread misinformation, and intimidate those who oppose the intended narrative. Trolls are effective at sowing discord and creating confusion, as they often use inflammatory language, personal attacks, and false information to provoke emotional reactions. By engaging with critics and detractors, trolls can derail discussions and shift the focus away from the original topic, making it difficult for meaningful debate to take place. They also work to silence dissent by harassing and intimidating users who challenge the propaganda narrative, creating a hostile environment that discourages opposition.

Amplifying Controversy and Division

Trolls are also used to amplify controversy and division, particularly on sensitive topics such as politics, religion, or social issues. By posting provocative comments and engaging in arguments, trolls can inflame tensions and create a sense of polarization. This tactic serves to divide the audience, making it harder for people to come together and challenge the propaganda message. The more polarized the conversation becomes, the easier it is for propagandists to manipulate public perception, as individuals are more likely to align with their "side" and reject opposing viewpoints. The goal is to create a chaotic and divisive environment in which the propaganda message gains traction amidst the noise.

Creating Fake Accounts for Credibility

Fake accounts, also known as sockpuppets, are profiles that are designed to appear as real individuals. These accounts are used to lend credibility to the propaganda message by making it seem like ordinary people are supporting the narrative. Fake accounts can post personal stories, share opinions, and engage in conversations, creating the impression that the message has genuine grassroots support. By interacting with real users and amplifying the propaganda content, fake accounts make the narrative appear more legitimate and widespread. This perceived authenticity makes the message more persuasive, as people are more likely to trust information that appears to come from their peers rather than from an official source.

Building Networks of Fake Accounts

To maximize their impact, propagandists often create networks of fake accounts that interact with one another, creating the illusion of a large community supporting the message. These networks can be used to coordinate the sharing of content, generate trending topics, and engage with real users, making the propaganda message appear more popular and credible. By using multiple fake accounts to comment on posts, share content, and engage in discussions, propagandists can create a sense of momentum around the narrative, encouraging real users to join in. The coordinated nature of these networks makes them highly effective at influencing perception and shaping public discourse.

Manipulating Social Media Algorithms

Bots, trolls, and fake accounts are also used to manipulate social media algorithms, which determine what content is shown to users based on engagement levels. By generating large volumes of likes, shares, and comments, these tools can trick the algorithm into prioritizing the propaganda content, ensuring that it reaches a wider audience. The more engagement the content receives, the more likely it is to be featured in trending sections or recommended to users, further amplifying its reach. By leveraging these tools to game the algorithm, propagandists can ensure that their message gains maximum visibility and influence.

Suppressing Opposing Voices

In addition to spreading propaganda, bots, trolls, and fake accounts can be used to suppress opposing voices and limit the reach of dissenting opinions. This can be done through mass reporting, where bots and fake accounts are used to flag content from critics as inappropriate or offensive, leading to its removal or the suspension of the user's account. Trolls can also engage in coordinated harassment campaigns, overwhelming critics with abusive comments and making it difficult for them to continue participating in the conversation. By silencing opposition, propagandists create an environment in which their message is the dominant narrative, with little room for alternative viewpoints.

Maintaining Anonymity and Avoiding Detection

One of the key advantages of using bots, trolls, and fake accounts is the ability to maintain anonymity and avoid detection. By hiding behind fake profiles, propagandists can spread their message without revealing their true identity, making it difficult for platforms or authorities to trace the source of the propaganda. To avoid detection, bots and fake accounts are often programmed to behave like real users—posting at irregular intervals, engaging with a variety of content, and interacting with other users in a natural way. This makes them harder to identify and allows them to operate for longer periods without being flagged or removed.

Using bots, trolls, and fake accounts to influence perception involves amplifying propaganda messages, creating echo chambers, disrupting conversations, intimidating critics, lending credibility through fake profiles, manipulating social media algorithms, suppressing opposing voices, and maintaining anonymity. These digital tools allow propagandists to shape public discourse, create the illusion of widespread support, and manipulate the perception of reality. By leveraging the power of social media and digital platforms, propagandists can ensure that their message reaches a wide audience, influences public opinion, and becomes the dominant narrative.

Chapter 20: Silencing Dissent: Countering Opposition and Reinforcing Control

No propaganda campaign is complete without strategies to counter resistance and maintain control. Once a narrative is established, it will inevitably face challenges from critics, dissenters, and those who seek to expose the truth. Effective propaganda requires not only the creation of an enemy but also the sustained effort to discredit opponents and silence dissent. Those who challenge the narrative pose a threat to the perceived legitimacy of the message and, by extension, the authority that promotes it.

Handling resistance involves a range of techniques, from discrediting critics by labeling them as unpatriotic or aligning them with the enemy to using smear campaigns that attack their credibility. By creating an environment where questioning the narrative is equated with betrayal, leaders can discourage dissent and ensure that the majority remains aligned with their message. Suppression of opposition is not only about attacking critics directly but also about creating a climate of fear that discourages others from speaking out.

Reinforcing the enemy narrative over time is equally important for maintaining control. The initial creation of an enemy is not enough; the threat must be kept alive and relevant. This is done by continuously highlighting new incidents, whether real or fabricated, that reinforce the danger posed by the enemy. Leaders must remind the public of the threat at every opportunity, using media, speeches, and public events to ensure that the perception of danger remains strong. By keeping the enemy narrative fresh and evolving, leaders can maintain public support, justify their actions, and prevent the public from becoming complacent or skeptical.

This chapter will explore practical methods for handling resistance, discrediting critics, and reinforcing the enemy narrative to maintain control over time. It will provide insights into how to create a climate that discourages dissent while ensuring that the enemy narrative remains a powerful tool for rallying support and maintaining authority.

Neutralizing Opposition: Handling Resistance and Critics

IN ANY PROPAGANDA CAMPAIGN, there will inevitably be resistance and critics who challenge the narrative and attempt to expose the truth. Effectively handling these opponents is crucial for maintaining control over public perception and ensuring that the intended message remains dominant. Propagandists use a variety of techniques to discredit critics, suppress dissent, and prevent alternative viewpoints from gaining traction. By neutralizing opposition, they can create an environment in which the propaganda message is accepted without question. Below are key strategies for handling resistance and critics.

Discrediting the Source

One of the most effective ways to handle critics is to discredit the source of the criticism. By attacking the credibility of those who oppose the narrative, propagandists can undermine their arguments without directly addressing them. This can be done by labeling critics as biased, corrupt, or having ulterior motives. For example, if a journalist publishes a story that contradicts the propaganda message, they might be accused of being aligned with the enemy or of spreading fake news. By questioning the integrity of the critic, propagandists can sow doubt in the minds of the audience, making it less likely that they will take the criticism seriously.

Labeling Critics as Traitors or Enemies

Another powerful technique is to label critics as traitors or enemies of the state. By framing dissent as an attack on the nation or the community, propagandists can create a hostile environment for those who oppose the narrative. This tactic plays on people's fear of being ostracized or punished for being disloyal. Critics are portrayed as undermining national unity or aiding the enemy, making their arguments seem dangerous and untrustworthy. By equating dissent with betrayal, propagandists can discourage others from speaking out and create a climate in which only the dominant narrative is accepted.

Deflecting and Redirecting the Conversation

When confronted with criticism, propagandists often use deflection and redirection to avoid directly addressing the issue. Instead of responding to the specific points raised by critics, they shift the conversation to a different topic that is more favorable to their narrative. For example, if the critic points out flaws in the propaganda message, the response might be to focus on the perceived threat posed by the enemy or to emphasize the importance of national security. This tactic serves to distract the audience from the criticism and refocus their attention on the core message of the propaganda, ensuring that the critic's arguments are sidelined.

Overwhelming Critics with Counterarguments

Another technique for handling resistance is to overwhelm critics with a flood of counterarguments, whether they are valid or not. By inundating critics with a barrage of information, statistics, or unrelated arguments, propagandists can make it difficult for them to respond effectively. This tactic, known as the "Gish gallop," is designed to exhaust the critic and create the impression that there is overwhelming evidence in support of the propaganda narrative. The audience, seeing the sheer volume of counterarguments, may be inclined to believe that the critic's position is weak or unfounded, even if the counterarguments are misleading or irrelevant.

Creating a False Consensus

Creating the illusion of widespread support for the propaganda narrative is an effective way to marginalize critics. By using bots, fake accounts, and loyal supporters to amplify the message, propagandists can create a false consensus, making it seem like the majority of people agree with the narrative. This perceived consensus makes critics appear to be in the minority, which can discourage others from joining them. People are more likely to align themselves with what they perceive to be the majority view, and by creating this illusion, propagandists can isolate critics and minimize their influence.

Engaging in Character Assassination

Character assassination is a tactic used to personally attack critics and undermine their credibility in the eyes of the public. This involves spreading rumors, digging up past mistakes, or using smear campaigns to damage the critic's reputation. By focusing on the personal flaws or alleged misdeeds of the critic, propagandists can divert attention away from the substance of their arguments. The goal is to make the critic seem untrustworthy or morally compromised, thereby discrediting their opposition to the propaganda narrative. This tactic is particularly effective when the critic is a public figure, as it can create a lasting negative impression that overshadows their message.

Using Fear and Intimidation

Fear and intimidation are powerful tools for suppressing dissent. Critics who challenge the propaganda narrative may be threatened with legal action, job loss, or personal harm. By creating a climate of fear, propagandists can silence critics and prevent others from speaking out. This intimidation may be overt, such as public threats or arrests, or more subtle, such as warnings delivered through intermediaries. The goal is to make the consequences of dissent so severe that critics are deterred from continuing their opposition. When people fear retribution, they are less likely to challenge the dominant narrative, ensuring that the propaganda message remains unchallenged.

Misrepresenting Critics' Arguments

A common tactic for handling resistance is to misrepresent or oversimplify the arguments of critics, making them easier to dismiss. This technique, known as creating a "straw man," involves distorting the critic's position to make it seem unreasonable or extreme. For example, if a critic raises concerns about government overreach, propagandists might misrepresent their argument as being against national security altogether. By attacking this distorted version of the argument, propagandists can make the critic's position appear foolish or dangerous, thereby discrediting it in the eyes of the audience. Misrepresentation serves to undermine the credibility of the critic and prevent the audience from considering their arguments seriously.

Delegitimizing Alternative Sources of Information

To prevent critics from gaining traction, propagandists work to delegitimize alternative sources of information, such as independent media, NGOs, or academics. By labeling these sources as biased, foreign-influenced, or untrustworthy, propagandists can discourage the audience from seeking out alternative viewpoints. If the audience believes that all credible information comes from the propagandist's sources, they are less likely to be swayed by the arguments of critics. This tactic also helps to create an information monopoly, where the propaganda narrative is the only one that is seen as legitimate.

Fostering Division Among Critics

A divide-and-conquer approach can be effective in neutralizing opposition. By fostering division among critics—highlighting differences in their viewpoints, goals, or affiliations—propagandists can weaken their collective influence. This can be done by emphasizing disagreements between different opposition groups or by promoting false information to create suspicion and mistrust. When critics are divided, they are less effective in challenging the propaganda narrative, and their efforts to resist are more likely to fail. Encouraging infighting ensures that critics remain fragmented, making it easier to maintain control over the narrative.

Handling resistance and critics involves discrediting the source, labeling critics as traitors, deflecting the conversation, overwhelming critics with counterarguments, creating a false consensus, engaging in character assassination, using fear and intimidation, misrepresenting arguments, delegitimizing alternative sources, and fostering division among critics. These tactics are designed to marginalize opposition, maintain control over the narrative, and ensure that the propaganda message remains dominant. By effectively neutralizing critics, propagandists can create an environment where dissent is discouraged, and the intended message is accepted without question.

Sustained Hostility: Reinforcing the Enemy Narrative Over Time

AN EFFECTIVE ENEMY narrative must be continually reinforced to maintain its impact and ensure that the target remains perceived as a threat. The initial portrayal of an enemy is only the beginning; for the propaganda to be successful, the narrative must evolve and adapt over time, keeping the audience engaged and ensuring that the perception of the enemy remains vivid and urgent. Reinforcing the enemy narrative involves a series of strategies designed to remind the audience of the ongoing threat, justify the actions taken against the enemy, and ensure that the fear and hatred of the enemy do not fade. Below are the key techniques for reinforcing the enemy narrative over time.

Highlighting New Incidents and Threats

One of the most effective ways to keep the enemy narrative alive is to highlight new incidents and threats, whether they are real, exaggerated, or fabricated. Each new event—such as a diplomatic disagreement, a military maneuver, or even a rumored plot—provides an opportunity to remind the audience of the enemy's supposed hostility. By consistently drawing attention to these incidents, propagandists create a sense of ongoing danger, reinforcing the idea that the enemy remains a significant threat. The audience is constantly reminded that the threat is not only real but also active and evolving, making it necessary to remain vigilant.

Using Media to Keep the Narrative in Focus

Media plays a crucial role in reinforcing the enemy narrative by ensuring that the message remains visible and relevant. News reports, editorials, and talk shows can be used to repeatedly bring up the enemy, discussing their actions, intentions, and potential dangers. Even when there are no significant new incidents to report, the media can revisit past events, analyze hypothetical scenarios, or discuss the enemy's perceived motivations. By keeping the enemy in the media spotlight, propagandists ensure that the audience remains focused on the threat, and any sense of complacency is avoided.

Repetition of Core Messages

Repetition is a fundamental principle of effective propaganda, and it is essential for reinforcing the enemy narrative. The core messages—such as the enemy being dangerous, aggressive, and untrustworthy—must be repeated frequently to ensure that they become deeply ingrained in the audience's consciousness. Slogans, phrases, and talking points should be consistently used by leaders, media figures, and supporters to create a unified narrative. The more often these messages are repeated, the more likely they are to be accepted as truth, even without evidence. Repetition ensures that the enemy narrative becomes part of the collective understanding, making it difficult for alternative perspectives to gain traction.

Linking the Enemy to Internal Problems

Another effective way to reinforce the enemy narrative is to link the enemy to internal problems, such as economic issues, social unrest, or security concerns. By blaming the enemy for domestic difficulties, propagandists can create a sense of personal impact, making the threat feel more immediate and relevant to the audience. For example, an economic downturn might be blamed on the enemy's actions, such as trade restrictions or cyberattacks. By drawing a direct connection between the enemy and the audience's hardships, propagandists ensure that the hatred and fear of the enemy are sustained, as people perceive the threat as affecting their daily lives.

Evoking Historical Grievances

Historical grievances are a powerful tool for reinforcing the enemy narrative. By reminding the audience of past conflicts, betrayals, or injustices committed by the enemy, propagandists can evoke long-standing resentments and fears. The use of historical examples creates a sense of continuity, suggesting that the enemy has always been a threat and that their current actions are simply part of an ongoing pattern. This historical framing makes it more difficult for the audience to view the enemy in a neutral or positive light, as the perception of hostility is deeply rooted in the nation's past experiences. The more often these historical grievances are brought up, the more the audience is reminded of why the enemy must be opposed.

Emphasizing the Moral Superiority of "Us" vs. "Them"

Reinforcing the enemy narrative also involves emphasizing the moral superiority of "us" versus "them." Propagandists portray the enemy as morally corrupt, evil, or inhumane, while depicting themselves as righteous and just. By framing the conflict as a struggle between good and evil, the enemy is dehumanized, and the audience is encouraged to view them as undeserving of sympathy or compassion. This moral framing not only justifies the actions taken against the enemy but also strengthens the audience's sense of identity and unity. The more often this moral contrast is highlighted, the more the audience is convinced of the legitimacy of their hostility toward the enemy.

Organizing Public Events and Rallies

Public events, such as rallies, speeches, and commemorations, are effective for reinforcing the enemy narrative and keeping the audience engaged. These events provide an opportunity for leaders to speak directly to the audience, reminding them of the threat posed by the enemy and the need for unity. By using powerful rhetoric, national symbols, and emotional appeals, these events create a sense of solidarity and shared purpose. They also serve as a platform for repeating core messages and introducing new developments in the enemy narrative. The collective experience of attending such events strengthens the audience's commitment to the cause and reinforces their perception of the enemy as a common threat.

Framing Defensive Actions as Necessary Measures

To sustain the enemy narrative, it is important to frame any actions taken against the enemy—such as military interventions, sanctions, or surveillance—as necessary defensive measures. Propagandists emphasize that these actions are taken to protect the nation from the enemy's aggression, reinforcing the perception of the enemy as a threat. By framing these actions as defensive rather than offensive, the audience is more likely to support them and view them as justified. This framing also serves to legitimize the ongoing conflict, ensuring that the audience remains committed to the cause and supportive of the government's actions.

Engaging Supporters to Spread the Message

Reinforcing the enemy narrative is not solely the responsibility of leaders and the media; engaging supporters to spread the message is also crucial. Supporters can be encouraged to share content on social media, participate in discussions, and challenge critics of the narrative. By involving the audience in the propaganda effort, propagandists create a sense of ownership and commitment among supporters. The more people actively participate in spreading the narrative, the more it becomes ingrained in the collective consciousness. Supporters also serve as amplifiers, ensuring that the message reaches a wider audience and that the perception of the enemy as a threat is maintained.

Adapting the Narrative to Changing Circumstances

Finally, reinforcing the enemy narrative requires adapting it to changing circumstances. As events unfold and new information becomes available, the narrative must be adjusted to remain relevant and credible. For example, if the enemy takes actions that appear conciliatory, propagandists may frame these actions as deceptive or insincere, suggesting that they are part of a larger strategy to lull the audience into a false sense of security. By adapting the narrative to fit new developments, propagandists can ensure that the enemy continues to be perceived as a threat, regardless of changing circumstances. This flexibility allows the narrative to endure and remain effective over time.

Reinforcing the enemy narrative over time involves highlighting new incidents, using media to keep the message in focus, repeating core messages, linking the enemy to internal problems, evoking historical grievances, emphasizing moral superiority, organizing public events, framing actions as defensive, engaging supporters, and adapting the narrative as needed. These strategies ensure that the perception of the enemy as a threat is sustained, the audience remains engaged, and the propaganda message remains dominant. By continually reinforcing the enemy narrative, propagandists can maintain control over public perception and ensure that the intended message shapes the audience's beliefs and behaviors.

Part 6: The Price of Manipulation: Consequences and Ethical Considerations

Every propaganda campaign that seeks to create an enemy comes with consequences—both intended and unintended. While portraying others as threats can unite a population, foster loyalty, and justify actions that might otherwise be questioned, the impact of these campaigns reaches far beyond their immediate goals. The creation of enemies can be a powerful tool for consolidating power, rallying people around a common cause, and distracting from internal problems. However, the social, political, and psychological effects of these campaigns are often profound and enduring, leaving behind a complex legacy that can shape a nation for generations.

The consequences of enemy creation are felt in the social, political, and psychological fabric of society, often leaving scars that endure long after the propaganda has achieved its purpose. Socially, these campaigns can lead to the marginalization, isolation, or persecution of certain groups, creating divisions that are difficult to heal. When a particular group is labeled as the enemy, the resulting atmosphere of fear and hatred can lead to discrimination, violence, and long-lasting prejudice. Relationships between communities are damaged, trust is eroded, and the social fabric is weakened. These divisions are often difficult to bridge, as the animosity created during the propaganda campaign continues to fester long after the campaign itself has ended.

Politically, enemy creation can be used to justify aggressive policies, both domestically and internationally. By portraying an external or internal group as a threat, leaders can rally public support for measures that might otherwise be seen as extreme, such as military action, increased surveillance, or the suppression of civil liberties. The enemy narrative allows those in power to present themselves as the defenders of the nation, positioning their actions as necessary for the safety and security of the population. This concentration of power often comes at the cost of individual freedoms and democratic principles, as dissent is labeled as unpatriotic and critics are silenced. In the long term, this can lead to authoritarianism, where the creation of enemies becomes a tool for maintaining control rather than addressing genuine threats.

Psychologically, the effects of enemy creation are deeply personal, as they shape how individuals perceive the world and interact with others. Propaganda that portrays a group as an existential threat instills fear, hatred, and suspicion, leading people to view those labeled as enemies as less than human. This dehumanization makes it easier for individuals to justify acts of violence, discrimination, or exclusion against the targeted group. Fear becomes a driving force, influencing behavior and decision-making in ways that benefit those in power. Over time, this psychological manipulation can create a culture of paranoia and intolerance, where people are constantly on edge, looking for threats, and mistrusting those around them. This kind of environment can be emotionally exhausting and damaging, leading to increased anxiety, stress, and even trauma.

In some cases, propaganda campaigns that seek to create enemies can backfire, leading to unintended harm to those who initiated them. When the enemy narrative becomes too extreme or when it is revealed that the threat was exaggerated or fabricated, public trust in leadership can be severely damaged. Case studies of propaganda backfiring demonstrate that manipulating public perception is not without risks. When people realize that they have been deceived, they may turn against those who misled them, leading to a loss of credibility and authority. Additionally, creating enemies can provoke retaliatory actions from the targeted group, leading to conflicts that escalate beyond the control of those who initiated the propaganda. The consequences of enemy creation are often unpredictable, and the use of fear and hatred as tools for manipulation can easily spiral out of control.

Alongside the consequences lie ethical considerations and moral implications. The use of propaganda to create enemies raises important questions about the morality of manipulation, deception, and the deliberate incitement of hatred. It challenges the ethical responsibilities of those who wield power and influence over public perception. Is it ever justifiable to manipulate the truth for the sake of unity or control? What are the moral limits of using fear to achieve political ends? These questions are particularly pressing in the context of enemy creation, where the consequences can include violence, persecution, and the loss of innocent lives. The ethical dilemmas posed by propaganda invite reflection on the responsibilities of leaders, the role of the media, and the impact of these campaigns on the lives of ordinary people.

The long-term impact of propaganda on society is significant and multifaceted. One of the most damaging effects is the erosion of trust—both in institutions and between individuals. When people realize that they have been manipulated, their trust in leadership, media, and even their fellow citizens can be shattered. This loss of trust makes it difficult to rebuild a sense of community and cooperation, as people become skeptical of information and hesitant to engage with others. The normalization of hate and the perpetuation of conflict are also long-term consequences of enemy creation. Once hatred is instilled, it can be passed down through generations, creating a cycle of animosity that is difficult to break. The legacy of propaganda can include not only social division and political instability but also a culture of intolerance and fear that undermines the possibility of peace and reconciliation.

Ultimately, the ethical and moral implications of using propaganda to create enemies force us to confront the kind of society we wish to create and the consequences we are willing to accept for achieving our goals. The manipulation of truth, the incitement of fear and hatred, and the deliberate targeting of certain groups for political gain all carry a heavy cost. While these tactics may offer short-term benefits for those in power, the long-term damage to the social fabric, political stability, and the psychological well-being of individuals cannot be ignored. As we explore the consequences and considerations of enemy creation, it is crucial to understand that the price of manipulation is often paid not only by the targets of propaganda but by society as a whole.

Chapter 21: The Ripple Effects: Consequences of Creating Enemies

The creation of an enemy is a powerful tool for those seeking to unite a group, justify their actions, or maintain control over a population. Throughout history, the practice of defining and targeting an enemy has been used to rally support, strengthen group identity, and divert attention from internal problems. However, the consequences of creating enemies are far-reaching and often complex, impacting society on multiple levels. The effects of enemy creation extend beyond the immediate objectives of the propagandist, leaving lasting scars on social, political, and psychological landscapes. These consequences are not always predictable or controllable, and what begins as a calculated effort to consolidate power or rally support can lead to unintended damage that reverberates across generations.

Socially, the process of enemy creation divides communities, fosters distrust, and legitimizes discrimination. When a particular group is labeled as an enemy, the fear and hatred generated can lead to social isolation, persecution, and even violence against that group. Prejudices are amplified, and relationships between different segments of society become strained. The act of defining an "us versus them" dynamic fractures communities, turning neighbors into adversaries and leading to deep-seated divisions that are difficult to heal. These divisions can persist long after the original propaganda campaign has ended, leaving communities polarized and incapable of reconciling their differences. The seeds of hatred sown by enemy creation can lead to generational trauma, where the animosity between groups is passed down and perpetuated.

Moreover, the targeting of a particular group as an enemy often legitimizes acts of discrimination and exclusion. People who are branded as the enemy may be denied rights, opportunities, and freedoms, leading to systemic inequality. Social cohesion suffers as mistrust grows, and individuals feel unsafe or unwelcome in their own communities. The long-term impact of such social fragmentation can manifest in ongoing conflicts, difficulties in achieving peace, and an inability to create inclusive and harmonious societies.

Politically, the portrayal of an enemy serves as a convenient justification for extreme measures. Leaders often use the narrative of a dangerous enemy to justify actions that would otherwise be deemed unacceptable, such as restricting civil liberties, increasing state control, or even launching military interventions. The fear generated by the enemy narrative allows those in power to consolidate authority, using the supposed threat to legitimize their decisions and maintain their grip on power. This manipulation of public fear often leads to the suppression of dissent, as criticism of the leadership can be framed as disloyalty or collaboration with the enemy.

In the long term, the political consequences of enemy creation can contribute to the erosion of democratic values and the rise of authoritarianism. When leaders use the enemy narrative to justify centralizing power and curtailing freedoms, they establish a precedent for future leaders to do the same. Citizens, conditioned to accept that such measures are necessary for their safety, may become more willing to trade freedom for security, allowing for the gradual dismantling of democratic institutions. The use of enemy narratives to concentrate power can also lead to a culture of fear and suspicion, in which people are afraid to express dissent or criticize the government.

Psychologically, enemy creation profoundly affects individuals, shaping how they perceive themselves, others, and the world. The narrative of an enemy instills fear, hatred, and a sense of constant threat, affecting the emotional and mental well-being of individuals. This psychological manipulation creates an environment where people view those labeled as enemies with suspicion and animosity, leading to dehumanization. When individuals are conditioned to see a particular group as inherently dangerous or inferior, they become more willing to justify acts of discrimination, violence, or exclusion against that group. The psychological toll of living in a state of constant fear and hatred can lead to increased levels of anxiety, stress, and even trauma.

The psychological impact of enemy creation extends beyond the targeted group to affect the general population as well. People who are repeatedly exposed to propaganda that emphasizes threats and dangers may develop a heightened sense of paranoia and mistrust, not only of the enemy but of others within their own community. This can lead to a breakdown in social relationships, as people become more isolated and less willing to engage with those who are different from themselves. The long-term consequences of such psychological manipulation include a culture of intolerance and division, where fear and hatred are normalized, and empathy and understanding are eroded.

Moreover, the creation of enemies is not without its risks, and propaganda campaigns can sometimes backfire, leading to unintended and often damaging consequences for those who initiated them. When the enemy narrative becomes too extreme, or when it is revealed that the threat was exaggerated or fabricated, public trust in leadership can be severely damaged. People who realize they have been deceived may turn against those who misled them, leading to social unrest, protests, and a loss of authority for the propagandists. The collapse of the enemy narrative can also lead to a sense of disillusionment and betrayal among the public, making it difficult for leaders to regain credibility and support.

There are numerous case studies throughout history that demonstrate the dangers of enemy creation backfiring. For example, during the Cold War, both the United States and the Soviet Union used propaganda to create fear of the other side, portraying their adversary as an existential threat. While this approach succeeded in rallying support for government policies and justifying military expenditures, it also led to a climate of paranoia and fear that contributed to social unrest and distrust of government institutions. In the United States, the Red Scare and McCarthyism, which sought to root out supposed communist sympathizers, led to widespread fear and suspicion, damaging the reputations and lives of countless innocent people. When it later became clear that many of these accusations were unfounded, public trust in government was eroded, and the political fallout was significant.

Similarly, during times of war, governments have often used enemy creation to justify military actions and rally public support. However, when the public learns that the justification for war was based on false or exaggerated information, the backlash can be severe. For instance, the Iraq War, which was justified in part by the claim that Iraq possessed weapons of mass destruction, led to significant political and social consequences when it was revealed that these claims were unfounded. The sense of betrayal felt by the public led to widespread protests, a loss of trust in government, and a long-term skepticism of official narratives, particularly regarding foreign policy.

The unintended consequences of enemy creation also extend to international relations. By framing another nation or group as an enemy, propagandists can provoke retaliatory actions that escalate into conflicts beyond their control. Diplomatic relations may be damaged, trade partnerships may be severed, and the risk of military confrontation may increase. The rhetoric used to create an enemy can make it difficult to de-escalate tensions, as leaders may become trapped in their own narratives, unable to back down without appearing weak or disingenuous. The consequences of such escalations can be devastating, leading to loss of life, economic hardship, and long-lasting hostility between nations.

Ultimately, the consequences of enemy creation are complex and multifaceted, affecting society, politics, and individual psychology in profound ways. While the creation of an enemy can serve short-term goals—such as uniting a population, consolidating power, or justifying policies—the long-term effects are often damaging and difficult to reverse. Social divisions, political authoritarianism, and psychological trauma are just some of the costs associated with this powerful yet dangerous tactic.

This chapter will delve into the social, political, and psychological effects of creating enemies, examining the real-world consequences that unfold when propaganda is used to manipulate perception and shape public opinion. By exploring case studies of propaganda campaigns that have backfired, it will also provide insight into the risks and unintended damage that can result from creating enemies. Understanding these consequences is crucial for recognizing the true power of propaganda and the responsibility that comes with wielding such influence over society.

Impact of Division: Social, Political, and Psychological Effects of Creating Enemies

THE CREATION OF ENEMIES through propaganda has profound social, political, and psychological effects, shaping the way societies function, altering power dynamics, and influencing individual behavior and thought. This practice, often used to rally support, consolidate power, or justify actions, can have far-reaching and long-lasting consequences that impact the very fabric of society. Below, the detailed effects of enemy creation are explored from social, political, and psychological perspectives.

Social Effects

The social effects of creating enemies are among the most immediate and visible consequences of propaganda. When a particular group is labeled as an enemy, it results in the division of society into "us" versus "them." Such divisions foster distrust, hatred, and fear between groups, leading to social fragmentation. People begin to perceive those labeled as enemies not as individuals but as representatives of a threatening "other," making it easier to justify discriminatory attitudes and actions.

This division often leads to the social isolation and marginalization of the targeted group. They may be excluded from public life, face systemic discrimination, or be denied basic rights and opportunities. The atmosphere of hostility and suspicion makes it difficult for members of the targeted group to integrate into society, leading to increased social tensions and even violence. These social divisions can become deeply entrenched, persisting long after the propaganda campaign has ended and making reconciliation and unity extremely challenging.

The breakdown of trust is another significant social consequence. Propaganda that creates enemies erodes the trust that individuals have in one another and in their communities. People become wary of those who are different, and relationships that were once based on mutual respect and understanding become strained. This lack of trust weakens social cohesion, making it difficult for communities to work together for the common good. The long-term impact of such social fragmentation can be devastating, leading to a society where prejudice, suspicion, and hatred become the norm.

Political Effects

Politically, the creation of enemies serves as a powerful tool for those in positions of authority. By portraying an external or internal group as a threat, leaders can rally support, justify extreme policies, and consolidate their power. The enemy narrative allows those in power to present themselves as protectors of the people, positioning their actions—whether they involve military intervention, surveillance, or the suppression of dissent—as necessary measures to ensure the security and stability of the nation.

The creation of an enemy can also serve as a distraction from internal issues. When the public is focused on a perceived external threat, they are less likely to scrutinize the actions of their own government or question domestic problems such as economic hardship, corruption, or social inequality. This redirection of attention allows leaders to avoid accountability and maintain control without addressing the underlying issues affecting their society.

However, the political consequences of creating enemies are not always beneficial for those in power. The fear and hatred generated by enemy narratives can spiral out of control, leading to unintended conflicts and instability. Leaders may find themselves trapped in the rhetoric they have created, unable to back down from aggressive policies without appearing weak. This can escalate tensions and lead to conflicts that are difficult to resolve. Additionally, when it becomes evident that the enemy narrative was based on false or exaggerated information, public trust in leadership can be severely damaged, leading to political unrest and a loss of legitimacy.

The long-term political impact of creating enemies can include the erosion of democratic principles. By using the enemy narrative to justify authoritarian measures, leaders may establish precedents that are difficult to reverse. Citizens conditioned to accept restrictions on their freedoms for the sake of security may become more willing to tolerate authoritarianism, leading to a gradual dismantling of democratic institutions. The use of enemy creation as a political tool ultimately undermines the principles of transparency, accountability, and respect for human rights that are essential for a healthy democracy.

Psychological Effects

The psychological effects of creating enemies are profound, affecting both individuals and the collective psyche of a society. On an individual level, the constant exposure to propaganda that emphasizes threats and dangers can lead to heightened anxiety, fear, and a sense of vulnerability. People may become preoccupied with the perceived threat, leading to a state of hypervigilance where they are always on the lookout for danger. This chronic stress can have serious consequences for mental health, contributing to issues such as anxiety disorders, depression, and even post-traumatic stress.

Propaganda that creates enemies also fosters hatred and hostility, which can have a dehumanizing effect. When people are conditioned to view a particular group as the enemy, they begin to see them not as individuals but as embodiments of a threat. This dehumanization makes it easier to justify acts of aggression, discrimination, or exclusion against the targeted group. The loss of empathy and understanding for those who are different can lead to a society where cruelty and intolerance are normalized, and acts of violence become more acceptable.

The psychological manipulation inherent in enemy creation also affects people's ability to think critically and make informed decisions. Propaganda often appeals to emotions rather than reason, using fear, anger, and pride to influence behavior. When individuals are constantly exposed to emotionally charged messages, their ability to evaluate information rationally is compromised. They may become more susceptible to accepting false or misleading information and less likely to question the actions of those in power. This undermines their autonomy and their ability to make independent choices based on accurate information.

On a collective level, the creation of enemies can lead to a culture of fear and suspicion. People become wary of those who are different, and the sense of community and solidarity that binds society together is weakened. The collective psyche becomes dominated by a siege mentality, where the outside world is viewed with suspicion, and the focus is on protecting oneself from perceived threats. This mindset makes it difficult for society to move beyond conflict, as the fear and hatred instilled by propaganda continue to influence attitudes and behaviors long after the original campaign has ended.

The creation of enemies also has generational psychological effects. Children who grow up in an environment where a particular group is labeled as an enemy are likely to internalize these beliefs, leading to the perpetuation of prejudice and hatred across generations. The narratives they are exposed to shape their worldview, making it difficult for them to see beyond the stereotypes and biases that have been ingrained in them. This perpetuation of hatred ensures that the divisions created by propaganda persist, making reconciliation and peace more challenging to achieve.

The social, political, and psychological effects of creating enemies are deeply interconnected, each reinforcing the other to create a cycle of division, fear, and control. The social fragmentation that results from enemy creation weakens communities and fosters prejudice, while the political manipulation of fear allows those in power to justify extreme measures and consolidate authority. The psychological toll of living in a state of constant fear and hostility affects individuals' mental health, their ability to think critically, and their relationships with others.

These effects are not easily reversed, and the damage caused by propaganda can persist long after the original campaign has ended. The consequences of creating enemies are far-reaching, impacting every aspect of society and leaving a legacy of division, mistrust, and resentment. Understanding these effects is crucial for recognizing the true cost of using propaganda as a tool for manipulation and for evaluating whether the short-term gains of enemy creation are worth the long-term harm inflicted on society.

Unintended Consequences: Case Studies of Propaganda Backfiring

PROPAGANDA IS OFTEN employed with the expectation that it will unify a population, justify a policy, or secure support for those in power. However, the manipulation of truth and the creation of enemies are not without risks, and history provides numerous examples of propaganda campaigns that have backfired, leading to unintended and often damaging consequences for those who initiated them. These case studies reveal that while propaganda can be a powerful tool, it is also a double-edged sword that can undermine the very goals it seeks to achieve.

The Red Scare and McCarthyism in the United States

One of the most notable examples of propaganda backfiring is the Red Scare and the rise of McCarthyism in the United States during the late 1940s and early 1950s. During this period, the American government, led by figures like Senator Joseph McCarthy, used propaganda to portray communism as an existential threat to the American way of life. Fear of communism was stoked through sensationalized media reports, exaggerated claims of communist infiltration, and public accusations against individuals alleged to be communists or communist sympathizers. This campaign successfully created a climate of fear and paranoia, leading to widespread support for aggressive measures to root out the perceived enemy.

However, the campaign ultimately backfired when the public became disillusioned with the lack of evidence to support many of the accusations. As more people began to see the extent of the false claims and the devastating impact they had on innocent individuals, public opinion turned against McCarthy and his supporters. The televised Army-McCarthy hearings in 1954 exposed McCarthy's tactics to the American public, revealing the baseless accusations and personal attacks that characterized his campaign. As a result, McCarthy lost credibility, and the term "McCarthyism" became synonymous with reckless and baseless persecution. The fallout from this propaganda campaign included a significant loss of trust in government institutions, widespread resentment, and a lasting legacy of suspicion and division within American society.

The Iraq War and Weapons of Mass Destruction

Another significant example of propaganda backfiring is the lead-up to the Iraq War in 2003. The U.S. government, along with its allies, used propaganda to create the narrative that Iraq possessed weapons of mass destruction (WMDs) and posed an imminent threat to global security. This narrative was used to justify the invasion of Iraq, and it was disseminated through speeches, media reports, and official statements that emphasized the danger posed by the Iraqi regime. The fear of WMDs was a powerful motivator, and the propaganda campaign successfully garnered public support for military action.

However, when it became clear that the evidence for Iraq's WMDs was either flawed or fabricated, the propaganda campaign began to unravel. The inability to find any WMDs in Iraq led to widespread criticism and accusations that the public had been deliberately misled. The realization that the justification for the war was based on false information led to a significant loss of trust in political leaders, both in the United States and abroad. The backlash included massive protests, a decline in public support for the war, and increased skepticism of government narratives in the years that followed. The long-term consequences of this propaganda backfire included political instability in the Middle East, a surge in anti-Western sentiment, and deep divisions within the countries that supported the war.

The Nazi Anti-Semitic Campaign and International Reaction

The Nazi regime in Germany used propaganda extensively to create an enemy out of the Jewish population, portraying Jews as a threat to German society and using anti-Semitic rhetoric to justify discriminatory laws, violence, and ultimately genocide. The propaganda campaign was highly effective in dehumanizing Jews and rallying much of the German population to support or tolerate increasingly extreme measures against them. However, the long-term consequences of this propaganda campaign ultimately backfired on the Nazi regime itself. As the extent of the atrocities committed against Jews and other marginalized groups during the Holocaust became known to the international community, the propaganda campaign backfired by generating widespread condemnation and horror. The revelations of concentration camps and the systemic extermination of millions of people led to a significant loss of legitimacy for the Nazi regime, even among some of its former supporters. The horrors of the Holocaust galvanized the international community to take action, leading to the establishment of the United Nations and the adoption of human rights principles designed to prevent such atrocities in the future. The Nazi propaganda campaign, which sought to unify the German people by creating a common enemy, instead led to Germany's vilification and isolation on the world stage for decades.

The Cultural Revolution in China

The Cultural Revolution in China, launched by Chairman Mao Zedong in 1966, provides another example of propaganda backfiring. Mao used propaganda to create an enemy out of perceived "bourgeois" elements within Chinese society, portraying them as a threat to the ideals of communism. Propaganda posters, speeches, and campaigns were used to rally the youth of China, known as the Red Guards, to attack intellectuals, party officials, and anyone deemed to be counter-revolutionary. The goal was to reassert Mao's control and eliminate opposition, using the creation of an internal enemy to galvanize support.

While the initial propaganda campaign succeeded in mobilizing millions of people, the consequences soon spiraled out of control. The Red Guards' fervor led to widespread chaos, violence, and the persecution of countless individuals, resulting in significant social and economic disruption. As the Cultural Revolution progressed, the lack of clear direction and the destructive behavior of the Red Guards began to undermine the stability of the country. By the early 1970s, Mao and the Communist Party were forced to rein in the very forces they had unleashed, as the social and economic consequences of the campaign became unsustainable. The Cultural Revolution left China deeply scarred, with a lost generation of young people whose education and futures had been disrupted, and it led to widespread disillusionment with Mao's leadership and the Communist Party.

Brexit and Anti-Immigration Propaganda

The 2016 Brexit referendum in the United Kingdom also serves as an example of propaganda backfiring. During the campaign, anti-immigration propaganda was used by proponents of leaving the European Union (EU) to create a narrative that portrayed immigrants as a threat to British jobs, culture, and security. Slogans like "Take Back Control" and misleading claims about the economic benefits of leaving the EU were employed to rally support for Brexit, tapping into fears about immigration and national sovereignty.

While the propaganda campaign succeeded in securing a majority vote to leave the EU, the aftermath revealed the unintended consequences of the narrative that had been created. The economic challenges and uncertainty that followed the referendum led to a significant decline in public trust in political leaders who had championed Brexit. Many of the promises made during the campaign, such as increased funding for the National Health Service (NHS), failed to materialize, leading to accusations that the public had been misled. The polarization and divisions created by the Brexit campaign have continued to affect British society, with ongoing debates about immigration, trade, and national identity. The initial success of the propaganda campaign in securing a "Leave" vote ultimately led to long-term political and social instability, highlighting the dangers of using fear-based narratives to achieve political goals.

These case studies illustrate that while propaganda can be an effective tool for creating enemies and rallying support, it is also fraught with risks and unintended consequences. When propaganda campaigns rely on deception, fear, and hatred, they can easily spiral out of control, leading to outcomes that are damaging not only to the targeted enemy but also to those who initiated the campaign. The backlash that often follows the exposure of falsehoods or the realization of the destructive impact of propaganda can lead to a loss of credibility, social unrest, and political instability.

The unintended consequences of propaganda reveal the dangers of manipulating public perception for short-term gain. The creation of enemies may offer a temporary boost in support or a means to justify extreme actions, but the long-term effects—social division, loss of trust, political backlash, and international condemnation—often outweigh the initial benefits. Understanding these case studies is crucial for recognizing the inherent risks of propaganda and the potential for it to backfire, ultimately undermining the very objectives it seeks to achieve.

Chapter 22: Moral Boundaries: The Ethics of Propaganda

Propaganda, especially when used to create an enemy, raises significant ethical questions about the use of manipulation, deception, and fear to achieve political or social objectives. It is a powerful tool that can influence minds, shape societies, and mobilize populations, but it comes with profound moral implications that must be examined. The use of propaganda to manipulate perception and incite hostility often involves a deliberate distortion of the truth, blurring the lines between right and wrong in the pursuit of a desired outcome. This chapter will explore the ethical considerations and moral implications of employing propaganda, particularly when it involves constructing an enemy narrative to unify or control a population.

At its core, the ethical debate around propaganda centers on the concept of truth and the responsibility of those who wield power over public perception. Is it ever justifiable to lie or deceive for the greater good? When does the need for unity or security outweigh the importance of honesty and transparency? Propaganda often presents a simplified version of reality, one that reduces complex issues to a battle between good and evil, "us" versus "them." This oversimplification not only distorts the truth but also undermines the audience's ability to make informed decisions, raising serious ethical concerns about the manipulation of free will. By choosing what information to present and what to omit, propagandists control the narrative, stripping individuals of the ability to think critically and form their own opinions.

The use of fear as a tool of control is particularly troubling from an ethical standpoint. Fear is a powerful emotion that can override reason, compelling people to act in ways they might not otherwise consider. Propaganda that creates an enemy often relies on stoking fear to unite people against a perceived threat. But is it ethical to use fear to manipulate behavior, even if the goal is to protect the community? Fear-based propaganda can lead people to support extreme measures, such as curtailing civil liberties, accepting authoritarian rule, or condoning violence. The ethical dilemma lies in the fact that these decisions are not made freely; they are coerced by fear, raising questions about the morality of using emotional manipulation to achieve political ends.

The moral implications extend beyond the act of deception itself. Propaganda that creates an enemy relies on inciting negative emotions—fear, hatred, and anger—towards a targeted group. By deliberately fostering these emotions, propagandists dehumanize the enemy and justify actions that may be unethical, such as discrimination, violence, or exclusion. The ethical question becomes: to what extent is it acceptable to incite hatred in the pursuit of political or social objectives? The dehumanization of others can have dire consequences, not only for the targeted group but for society as a whole, as it erodes empathy, tolerance, and the capacity for understanding. The deliberate incitement of hatred risks normalizing violence and division, creating an environment where cruelty and aggression are accepted, if not encouraged.

Another ethical issue concerns the role of leaders and the responsibilities they hold. Leaders who use propaganda to create enemies are exploiting their positions of power to manipulate those they are supposed to serve. Their role should be to inform, protect, and unify their people, not to deceive and divide them for political gain. When leaders choose to create an enemy, they are prioritizing their own interests over the well-being of the society they govern. This abuse of power is inherently unethical, as it undermines the social contract between the governed and those in positions of authority. Ethical leadership requires transparency, accountability, and a commitment to the truth, even when it is inconvenient or unpopular.

The role of the media in disseminating propaganda also raises ethical questions. Media outlets have a responsibility to provide accurate and balanced information to the public. However, when they become complicit in spreading propaganda, they betray this responsibility, contributing to the manipulation of public perception. The ethical implications of media involvement in propaganda are significant, as the media serves as a gatekeeper of information. When it chooses to amplify certain messages and silence others, it shapes the narrative in ways that can have profound effects on society. The ethical responsibility of the media is to serve as a check on power, not as a tool of manipulation. When this responsibility is compromised, the consequences for democracy and public trust are severe.

The long-term impact of propaganda on society is another crucial ethical consideration. Propaganda leaves a lasting imprint on social norms, political systems, and individual psychology. It can create divisions that persist long after the initial campaign has ended, fostering a culture of intolerance, suspicion, and hostility. The normalization of hate and the acceptance of manipulated truths undermine the foundations of a healthy society, making it difficult to rebuild trust and promote reconciliation. These long-term consequences raise questions about the morality of using propaganda as a tool for short-term gain, especially when the price is the erosion of social cohesion and the perpetuation of conflict.

One of the most damaging long-term effects of propaganda is the erosion of trust—both in institutions and between individuals. When people realize that they have been manipulated, their trust in leadership, the media, and even their fellow citizens is shattered. This loss of trust makes it difficult to foster a sense of community and cooperation, as people become skeptical of the information they receive and hesitant to engage with others. The distrust that results from propaganda creates a fragmented society where individuals feel isolated and disconnected from one another. The rebuilding of trust is a slow and difficult process, and the damage caused by propaganda can take generations to heal.

Another long-term impact of propaganda is the perpetuation of prejudice and discrimination. The creation of an enemy narrative often relies on stereotypes and misinformation that paint a targeted group as dangerous, inferior, or untrustworthy. These stereotypes can become deeply ingrained in the public consciousness, leading to systemic discrimination that persists even after the propaganda campaign has ended. The ethical implications of perpetuating such prejudice are profound, as it leads to the marginalization of certain groups and the denial of their rights and dignity. A society that is built on discrimination and exclusion cannot be considered ethical or just.

The ethical considerations of propaganda also extend to its impact on the individual level. The use of manipulation and deception to control people's beliefs and behaviors is inherently unethical, as it strips individuals of their autonomy and their right to make informed decisions. Propaganda takes advantage of psychological vulnerabilities, exploiting people's fears, desires, and insecurities to achieve a desired outcome. This kind of manipulation is a violation of individual rights, as it denies people the ability to think critically and to make choices based on accurate information. The moral implications of such manipulation are significant, as they challenge the fundamental principles of respect for human dignity and autonomy.

In examining the ethics of propaganda, it is important to reflect on the responsibilities of leaders, the role of the media, and the impact of these tactics on individuals and communities. Ethical leadership requires a commitment to the truth, transparency, and the well-being of the people. Leaders who use propaganda to create enemies are prioritizing their own interests over the common good, an inherently unethical act that undermines the trust and cohesion of society. The media, as a powerful force in shaping public perception, also has an ethical responsibility to provide accurate and balanced information, rather than becoming a tool of manipulation.

Ultimately, the ethical and moral implications of using propaganda to create enemies force us to confront the kind of society we wish to create and the consequences we are willing to accept for achieving our goals. The manipulation of truth, the incitement of fear and hatred, and the deliberate targeting of certain groups for political gain all carry a heavy cost. While these tactics may offer short-term benefits for those in power, the long-term damage to the social fabric, political stability, and the psychological well-being of individuals cannot be ignored. Propaganda, when used unethically, leaves a trail of division, mistrust, and resentment that undermines the possibility of building a just and cohesive society.

This chapter will delve into the ethical dilemmas surrounding the use of propaganda, exploring both the moral arguments for and against its use and the long-term effects it has on society. It will examine the responsibilities of those who wield power, the impact of propaganda on public trust, and the ethical limits of using manipulation to achieve political or social ends. By understanding the ethical implications, it becomes possible to evaluate the true cost of employing propaganda to create enemies and to question whether the ends truly justify the means. It invites reflection on the choices that leaders, the media, and individuals must make in the pursuit of power and influence, and whether those choices align with the values of truth, justice, and respect for human dignity.

Moral Dilemmas: Ethical Considerations and Moral Implications

THE USE OF PROPAGANDA to create enemies raises significant ethical concerns and moral dilemmas. While propaganda can be an effective means of unifying a population, rallying support, and justifying actions, it often comes at the cost of truth, integrity, and respect for individual rights. The ethical considerations surrounding propaganda revolve around issues of manipulation, deception, and the deliberate incitement of fear and hatred, which can have damaging effects on both individuals and society as a whole.

One of the primary ethical concerns with using propaganda to create enemies is the deliberate manipulation of information. Propaganda often involves presenting a distorted version of reality, selecting certain facts while omitting others, or using emotionally charged language to influence public perception. This manipulation undermines individuals' ability to make informed decisions, as they are being fed a narrative that may not reflect the full truth. The ethical question here is whether it is ever justifiable to deceive people for a perceived greater good. Is it acceptable to deny individuals the right to access accurate information and form their own opinions, simply to achieve a specific political or social outcome?

Another ethical issue is the use of fear as a tool of control. Propaganda that creates enemies often relies on instilling fear in the population, portraying the enemy as an imminent threat that must be confronted. Fear is a powerful motivator, but it also bypasses rational thought, compelling people to act in ways they might not otherwise consider. When fear is used to manipulate behavior, individuals are not acting out of free will; they are being coerced into supporting policies or actions that they may not fully understand or agree with. The use of fear to control a population raises serious ethical questions about the legitimacy of such tactics and the moral responsibility of those who employ them.

The incitement of hatred and hostility towards a targeted group is another major ethical concern. Propaganda that creates enemies often dehumanizes the targeted group, portraying them as dangerous, inferior, or inherently evil. This dehumanization serves to justify acts of discrimination, violence, and exclusion, as the enemy is no longer seen as deserving of empathy or compassion. The ethical implications of inciting hatred are profound, as it not only harms the targeted group but also erodes the moral fabric of society. A society built on hatred and division is one in which tolerance, understanding, and coexistence are compromised, leading to long-term social instability and suffering.

The moral implications of propaganda also extend to the impact it has on individual autonomy. The use of propaganda to influence people's beliefs and behaviors is inherently unethical because it strips individuals of their ability to make informed, independent choices. By manipulating emotions and controlling the flow of information, propagandists are effectively denying people their right to think critically and decide for themselves. This violation of autonomy is a fundamental ethical issue, as it disrespects the dignity and rights of individuals as rational beings capable of making their own decisions.

The responsibilities of leaders who use propaganda to create enemies are also an important ethical consideration. Leaders have a duty to act in the best interests of those they govern, which includes providing accurate information, promoting unity, and protecting the rights of all citizens. When leaders choose to use propaganda to create enemies, they are prioritizing their own interests—whether it be maintaining power, diverting attention from domestic issues, or justifying controversial actions—over the well-being of the population. This abuse of power is inherently unethical, as it undermines the trust that should exist between leaders and the people they serve. Ethical leadership requires transparency, accountability, and a commitment to truth, even when it is inconvenient or unpopular.

The role of the media in disseminating propaganda also raises significant ethical questions. The media is supposed to serve as a check on power, providing the public with accurate, balanced information and holding those in authority accountable. However, when the media becomes complicit in spreading propaganda, it betrays this responsibility and becomes a tool of manipulation. The ethical implications of media involvement in propaganda are profound, as the media has the power to shape public perception and influence the course of society. When it chooses to amplify certain messages and silence others, it contributes to the manipulation of public opinion and the erosion of trust in information sources.

Another ethical consideration is the long-term impact of propaganda on society. Propaganda that creates enemies leaves a lasting imprint, contributing to social division, political instability, and the perpetuation of prejudice and hatred. The normalization of hate and the acceptance of manipulated truths undermine the foundations of a healthy society, making it difficult to rebuild trust and promote reconciliation. The consequences of propaganda are often felt long after the original campaign has ended, affecting future generations and creating barriers to peace and unity. The moral question is whether the short-term benefits of using propaganda—such as rallying support or consolidating power—are worth the long-term damage inflicted on the social fabric of society.

The ethical dilemmas surrounding propaganda also invite reflection on the kind of society we wish to create and the values we hold dear. A society that relies on manipulation, deception, and the creation of enemies to achieve its goals is one in which truth, justice, and respect for human dignity are compromised. The use of propaganda to create enemies is fundamentally at odds with the principles of democracy, human rights, and social justice. It raises questions about the moral limits of political and social action and challenges us to consider whether the ends truly justify the means.

In conclusion, the ethical considerations and moral implications of using propaganda to create enemies are complex and far-reaching. The deliberate manipulation of information, the use of fear and hatred as tools of control, the violation of individual autonomy, the abuse of power by leaders, and the complicity of the media all raise serious ethical concerns. The long-term impact of propaganda on society—its contribution to division, distrust, and the perpetuation of prejudice—further underscores the moral cost of these tactics. By examining these ethical dilemmas, we can better understand the true cost of using propaganda and question whether it is ever justifiable to sacrifice truth, integrity, and respect for human rights in the pursuit of political or social objectives.

Lasting Shadows: The Long-Term Impact of Propaganda on Society

THE EFFECTS OF PROPAGANDA extend far beyond the immediate objectives of influencing public opinion or rallying support for a cause. Its consequences are long-lasting, shaping societal norms, political landscapes, and individual behaviors for generations. Propaganda, particularly when used to create enemies, leaves a profound mark on society that is difficult to erase. The long-term impact of such campaigns can be seen in the perpetuation of social division, the erosion of trust, the normalization of prejudice, and the undermining of democratic values.

One of the most significant long-term impacts of propaganda is the social division it creates. When a group is portrayed as the enemy, the resulting fear, suspicion, and hatred often lead to deep societal divides. These divisions can persist long after the original propaganda campaign has ended, as the stereotypes and biases instilled in people's minds become entrenched. The "us versus them" mentality promoted by propaganda fosters an environment where different groups are seen as fundamentally opposed, leading to isolation, segregation, and, in some cases, open conflict. The legacy of this division can be seen in ongoing ethnic, religious, or political tensions that have their roots in past propaganda campaigns.

The erosion of trust is another long-term consequence of propaganda. When people are repeatedly exposed to manipulated information and narratives designed to influence their beliefs, their trust in institutions, leaders, and even their fellow citizens begins to deteriorate. This loss of trust can have far-reaching implications for the functioning of society. Institutions such as the government, the media, and the judiciary rely on public trust to operate effectively, and when that trust is undermined, their legitimacy is called into question. The skepticism that results from the realization that propaganda has been used to deceive creates a society where people are less willing to believe in the credibility of information, making it difficult to foster cooperation, dialogue, and collective action.

Propaganda also contributes to the normalization of prejudice and discrimination, which can have a lasting impact on societal attitudes and behaviors. When a group is consistently portrayed as dangerous, inferior, or untrustworthy, these messages become internalized by the population, leading to systemic discrimination. This prejudice is often passed down from one generation to the next, making it difficult to overcome the biases and stereotypes that have been instilled through propaganda. The long-term impact is a society where certain groups are marginalized and denied equal rights and opportunities, perpetuating cycles of inequality and injustice.

The psychological impact of propaganda on individuals is another long-term effect that must be considered. Propaganda that creates enemies often relies on instilling fear and hatred, emotions that can have a profound effect on a person's mental health and worldview. The constant exposure to fear-based messaging can lead to anxiety, stress, and even trauma, affecting how individuals perceive themselves and others. The dehumanization of the enemy that is central to propaganda campaigns also erodes empathy and compassion, making it easier for individuals to justify acts of discrimination or violence against those who have been labeled as the enemy. The long-term psychological impact of propaganda is a society where fear and hatred are normalized, and where people are less likely to engage with others in a spirit of understanding and cooperation.

The political consequences of propaganda also have long-term implications for society. Propaganda is often used by those in power to justify extreme measures, such as restricting civil liberties, increasing surveillance, or even going to war. These measures, once accepted by the population, can become normalized, making it difficult to roll back authoritarian policies even after the perceived threat has passed. The use of propaganda to create enemies can lead to a culture of fear and control, where dissent is suppressed, and the population is conditioned to accept the concentration of power in the hands of a few. This undermines democratic values and principles, such as transparency, accountability, and respect for individual rights, creating a society that is more susceptible to authoritarianism.

Another long-term impact of propaganda is the creation of a culture of misinformation. When propaganda is used to manipulate public perception, it blurs the line between truth and falsehood, making it difficult for people to distinguish between fact and fiction. This culture of misinformation can have lasting effects, as individuals become more susceptible to believing false or misleading information. The spread of misinformation undermines informed decision-making, as people are less able to access accurate information and form their own opinions. This can lead to a society where critical thinking is discouraged, and where people are more easily manipulated by those in power.

The long-term impact of propaganda also extends to international relations. Propaganda that creates enemies often involves the demonization of other nations or groups, leading to increased hostility and tensions on the global stage. These tensions can persist long after the original propaganda campaign has ended, making it difficult for countries to build positive relationships and work together to address common challenges. The legacy of propaganda can include long-standing animosities between nations, a reluctance to engage in diplomacy, and an increased risk of conflict. The international mistrust fostered by propaganda can hinder cooperation on issues such as trade, security, and climate change, ultimately affecting the well-being of people around the world.

The economic impact of propaganda is another long-term consequence that should not be overlooked. Propaganda campaigns that create enemies can lead to economic isolation, as targeted groups or nations are subjected to sanctions, boycotts, or exclusion from economic opportunities. The economic marginalization of certain groups within a society can lead to cycles of poverty and inequality that are difficult to break. On a national level, the economic consequences of propaganda-driven conflict can include reduced foreign investment, disruptions to trade, and increased military spending, all of which can have a negative impact on a country's long-term economic stability and growth.

The legacy of propaganda is one that leaves lasting shadows over society. The divisions it creates, the mistrust it fosters, the prejudice it normalizes, and the values it undermines all contribute to a society that is less cohesive, less just, and less capable of addressing the challenges it faces. The long-term impact of propaganda is a society that is fractured, where fear and hatred are pervasive, and where the truth is obscured by misinformation and manipulation.

Understanding the long-term consequences of propaganda is crucial for recognizing the true cost of using such tactics to achieve short-term goals. While propaganda may offer immediate benefits for those seeking power or control, the damage it inflicts on the social fabric, political institutions, and individual well-being is often irreversible. The legacy of propaganda is one of division, distrust, and resentment—consequences that can take generations to overcome. By recognizing these long-term impacts, societies can better appreciate the importance of truth, transparency, and ethical leadership in building a future that is based on unity, understanding, and respect for all.

The Final Reflection: Power, Impact, and Responsibility of Propaganda

Propaganda is a powerful force that has shaped human history, molded public perception, and influenced the course of societies across the world. From the crafting of enemy narratives to the use of fear, misinformation, and emotional appeals, the techniques of propaganda have been employed to rally support, consolidate power, and manipulate entire populations. However, the true measure of propaganda lies not only in its immediate effectiveness but also in its lasting impact on society, leadership, and the individuals it touches.

The journey through the world of propaganda reveals the diverse techniques used to create enemies and achieve political or social goals. Simplifying complex issues, appealing to base emotions, spreading misinformation, and leveraging media channels are all essential tools in the propagandist's toolkit. These techniques are designed to bypass critical thinking, evoke strong emotional responses, and sway public opinion in a desired direction. However, the consequences of these methods extend beyond the immediate goals—shaping society in profound and often damaging ways.

The impact of creating enemies through propaganda is seen in the social, political, and psychological fabric of society. It divides communities, fosters hatred, erodes trust, and undermines the values of democracy and individual autonomy. The long-term effects of propaganda can lead to a fragmented society, where fear and prejudice become ingrained, and where democratic principles are compromised in the pursuit of power. Leaders who use propaganda must grapple with the ethical implications of their actions, recognizing that the consequences of manipulating truth and inciting hatred can be far-reaching and difficult to control.

Reflecting on the power of propaganda is also a call to consider the responsibility that comes with wielding such influence. The ability to shape perceptions, control narratives, and mobilize people is a significant power, one that requires a careful balance between achieving goals and respecting the rights and dignity of individuals. Propaganda, when used unethically, can leave a legacy of division, mistrust, and conflict—consequences that may take generations to heal. Understanding the full spectrum of propaganda's power, its techniques, its impact, and its moral considerations, allows for a deeper appreciation of both its potential and the weight of the responsibility it carries.

Techniques of Influence: Summary of Key Propaganda Methods

PROPAGANDA, AS A TOOL of influence, employs a range of techniques designed to shape public perception, control narratives, and manipulate emotions. These methods are carefully crafted to achieve specific outcomes—whether it is to unite people against a common enemy, rally support for a cause, or consolidate power in the hands of leaders. The key propaganda techniques can be categorized into various approaches that exploit human psychology and leverage media channels to maximize impact.

Enemy Creation and Dehumanization

One of the most powerful propaganda techniques is the creation of an enemy. By portraying a particular group as dangerous, evil, or a threat to society, propagandists create an "us versus them" dynamic that serves to unify the population against a common foe. This often involves dehumanizing the enemy, stripping them of individual identity and portraying them as a monolithic force that must be opposed. Dehumanization makes it easier to justify discrimination, violence, and exclusion, as the enemy is no longer seen as deserving of empathy or compassion.

Appeal to Fear

Fear is a fundamental human emotion that can override rational thought and drive people to take extreme actions. Propaganda often uses fear to create a sense of urgency and danger, convincing the audience that immediate action is necessary to protect themselves or their community. This can involve exaggerating threats, fabricating dangers, or using emotionally charged language to instill panic. The goal is to make people feel vulnerable and dependent on those in power for protection, thereby gaining their support for policies or actions they might otherwise oppose.

Misinformation and Disinformation

Misinformation—spreading false or misleading information—is a cornerstone of propaganda. This technique involves presenting information that appears credible but is either incomplete, distorted, or outright false. Disinformation, a subset of misinformation, is deliberately fabricated to deceive the audience. By controlling the flow of information and spreading lies, propagandists can create confusion, shape public perception, and undermine the credibility of opponents. Misinformation can be used to manipulate narratives, deflect attention from inconvenient truths, or create a false consensus in favor of a particular viewpoint.

Repetition of Core Messages

Repetition is a simple yet effective propaganda technique that involves repeating core messages over and over until they become ingrained in the minds of the audience. By constantly reiterating key phrases, slogans, or ideas, propagandists make these messages familiar, and familiarity breeds acceptance. The more a message is repeated, the more likely people are to believe it, even if it lacks evidence or logical reasoning. Repetition helps to create a sense of inevitability and legitimacy around the narrative being promoted.

Emotional Appeals

Propaganda frequently relies on emotional appeals rather than rational arguments. By tapping into emotions such as fear, anger, pride, or sympathy, propagandists can bypass critical thinking and motivate people to act based on their feelings. Emotional appeals make the message more relatable and memorable, encouraging people to share it with others and rally around the cause. By evoking strong emotions, propagandists create a sense of personal connection to the message, making it more difficult for individuals to question or reject it.

Simplification and Stereotyping

Complex issues are often reduced to simple narratives in propaganda, making it easier for people to understand and accept the message. This simplification often involves stereotyping, where groups of people are labeled with broad, generalized characteristics that define them as either good or bad. By simplifying complex social or political issues into binary terms—such as good versus evil or right versus wrong—propagandists remove nuance and ambiguity, making it easier for the audience to align themselves with the desired position.

Use of Symbols and Imagery

Symbols, imagery, and visual elements are powerful tools in propaganda, as they can convey complex messages in an easily digestible form. National flags, religious symbols, and powerful visuals that evoke pride, fear, or hatred are often used to reinforce the propaganda narrative. These symbols tap into deep-seated emotions and cultural associations, making the message resonate more strongly with the audience. Visual propaganda, such as posters, videos, and graphics, is especially effective in creating a lasting impression that reinforces the desired message.

Control of Information and Media

The control of information and the use of media channels are central to effective propaganda. By controlling what information is disseminated, how it is presented, and who has access to it, propagandists can shape public perception and limit exposure to alternative viewpoints. State-controlled media, selective reporting, censorship, and the amplification of favorable narratives are all techniques used to ensure that the desired message reaches the audience while dissenting voices are silenced or marginalized. The use of media to create echo chambers—where only one viewpoint is heard—ensures that the propaganda narrative becomes the dominant one.

Scapegoating and Blame Shifting

Scapegoating is a technique where a particular group is blamed for society's problems, thereby diverting attention away from the real causes and those in power. By blaming an external or internal enemy for issues such as economic hardship, social unrest, or security threats, propagandists can unify the population against a common target and deflect criticism from themselves. Scapegoating provides a simple explanation for complex problems, making it an appealing narrative for the audience and creating an outlet for frustration and anger.

Creating a False Consensus

Another key technique is the creation of a false consensus, which involves making it appear that the majority of people support the propagandist's narrative. This can be achieved through the use of fake accounts, bots, and media amplification to create the illusion of widespread agreement. By creating a sense that "everyone" supports a particular viewpoint, propagandists can pressure individuals into conforming, as people are often influenced by what they perceive to be the majority opinion. The perception of consensus can discourage dissent and make individuals more likely to accept the propaganda message.

These key propaganda techniques—enemy creation, appeal to fear, misinformation, repetition, emotional appeals, simplification, use of symbols, control of information, scapegoating, and creating a false consensus—are all designed to influence, manipulate, and control public perception. They exploit human psychology, leverage media platforms, and rely on emotional manipulation to achieve their goals. Understanding these methods provides insight into how propaganda operates and the power it has to shape societies, influence leadership, and impact individual thought and behavior. Recognizing these techniques is the first step in resisting manipulation and ensuring that decisions are made based on truth and reason rather than fear and deception.

Divided Societies and Empowered Leaders: The Impact of Creating Enemies

THE DELIBERATE CREATION of enemies through propaganda has far-reaching consequences that affect both society and leadership. This strategy, often used to consolidate power, control the population, or justify controversial actions, leaves an indelible mark on the social fabric and the dynamics of governance. By portraying a group, nation, or ideology as a threat, leaders can rally support, manipulate emotions, and achieve short-term goals. However, the long-term impacts of creating enemies are often deeply damaging, leading to societal division, erosion of trust, and shifts in political power.

One of the most significant impacts of creating enemies is the social division it causes. When a particular group is labeled as an enemy, it becomes the target of fear, suspicion, and hatred. This division fosters an "us versus them" mentality, where society is split into opposing camps, each viewing the other with distrust. Such divisions create a hostile environment in which different communities are pitted against each other, leading to segregation, discrimination, and even violence.

The resulting animosity can persist long after the propaganda campaign has ended, making it difficult to rebuild social cohesion and fostering ongoing conflict between groups.

The labeling of an enemy also has a profound effect on the marginalized group itself. Members of the targeted group often face systemic discrimination, exclusion from opportunities, and violations of their rights. The dehumanization that accompanies enemy creation serves to justify these actions, as the enemy is no longer seen as deserving of empathy or fair treatment. This marginalization can lead to cycles of poverty, inequality, and social unrest, as the targeted group struggles to overcome the barriers placed before them. The long-term effect is a fragmented society where certain groups are perpetually disadvantaged and isolated.

The psychological impact on society is another significant consequence of creating enemies. Propaganda that emphasizes threats and dangers instills fear and paranoia in the population. People begin to see those labeled as enemies not as individuals but as threats to their safety and well-being. This constant state of fear affects mental health, contributing to anxiety, stress, and a heightened sense of vulnerability. The hatred and hostility generated by enemy narratives also erode empathy and compassion, making it easier for individuals to justify acts of aggression or exclusion. The psychological toll of living in a society shaped by fear and division can lead to long-lasting emotional scars and a culture of intolerance.

On a political level, the creation of enemies is a powerful tool for leadership, allowing those in power to consolidate authority and control the population. By portraying themselves as protectors against a dangerous threat, leaders can rally support and justify actions that might otherwise be seen as extreme or unjust. The enemy narrative allows leaders to present themselves as defenders of the people, positioning their policies as necessary for the security and stability of the nation. This often leads to increased public support for authoritarian measures, such as surveillance, censorship, or restrictions on civil liberties, as the population is willing to trade freedom for perceived safety.

The creation of enemies also serves to deflect attention from internal problems, such as economic difficulties, corruption, or political scandals. When the population is focused on an external threat, they are less likely to scrutinize the actions of their leaders or question the state of their own society. This redirection of attention allows leaders to maintain power without addressing the underlying issues affecting their country. The enemy becomes a convenient scapegoat, blamed for the nation's problems and used to divert criticism from those in authority.

However, the impact of creating enemies is not always beneficial for leaders, and the strategy can backfire. When the enemy narrative becomes too extreme or when it is revealed that the perceived threat was exaggerated or fabricated, public trust in leadership can be severely damaged. People may feel betrayed when they realize they have been manipulated, leading to social unrest, protests, and a loss of legitimacy for those in power. Additionally, the hostility generated by enemy narratives can escalate into conflicts that spiral beyond the control of leaders, leading to unintended consequences that undermine their authority.

The long-term political impact of creating enemies can include the erosion of democratic values. The use of enemy narratives to justify authoritarian measures sets a precedent for future leaders to do the same. Citizens conditioned to accept restrictions on their freedoms for the sake of security may become more willing to tolerate authoritarianism, leading to a gradual dismantling of democratic institutions. The concentration of power in the hands of leaders who use propaganda to create enemies can result in a political culture where dissent is not tolerated, and the population is kept in a state of fear and dependence.

The international consequences of creating enemies should also be considered. Propaganda that portrays other nations or groups as enemies can lead to increased tensions and hostility on the global stage. This can hinder diplomatic efforts, reduce opportunities for cooperation, and increase the risk of conflict. The legacy of enemy creation can include long-standing animosities between nations, making it difficult to establish positive relationships and work together on global challenges. The international mistrust fostered by enemy narratives can have a lasting impact on a nation's ability to engage in constructive diplomacy and maintain peace.

The creation of enemies through propaganda has profound and lasting effects on both society and leadership. It divides communities, fosters hatred, and erodes empathy, creating a fragmented social fabric that is difficult to mend. Politically, it allows leaders to consolidate power, justify extreme measures, and deflect attention from internal issues, but it also carries the risk of backfiring and undermining trust in leadership. The long-term consequences of creating enemies are often deeply damaging, leading to the erosion of democratic values, increased authoritarianism, and persistent conflict both within and between nations. Understanding these impacts is crucial for recognizing the true cost of using propaganda as a tool for control and manipulation.

The Weight of Influence: A Reflection on the Power and Responsibility of Propaganda

PROPAGANDA HOLDS IMMENSE power—the ability to shape thoughts, manipulate emotions, and influence the actions of entire populations. It can be used to unify a nation in times of crisis, rally support for a cause, or even inspire significant social change. However, with such power comes a profound responsibility. The impact of propaganda extends far beyond its immediate objectives, affecting the social fabric, political dynamics, and individual lives in ways that can be both constructive and destructive. Reflecting on the power and responsibility of propaganda reveals the delicate balance between achieving desired outcomes and maintaining ethical integrity.

The power of propaganda lies in its ability to control the narrative. By deciding what information is presented, how it is framed, and who receives it, propagandists have the capacity to create a shared reality for their audience. This power can be used for positive purposes—mobilizing people to support humanitarian efforts, encouraging solidarity in times of national emergency, or fostering a sense of pride and belonging. However, it can just as easily be used for malicious purposes—creating enemies, inciting hatred, or justifying acts of aggression. The ability to control the narrative means that those who wield propaganda have the power to shape public perception and influence behaviors on a massive scale.

The responsibility that comes with the use of propaganda is significant. The deliberate manipulation of information, the creation of fear and hatred, and the use of deception all raise serious ethical questions. When leaders or media outlets use propaganda, they must consider the potential consequences of their actions—not just in the short term, but also the long-term impact on society. The effects of propaganda can include social division, the erosion of trust, the normalization of prejudice, and the undermining of democratic values. The responsibility of those who use propaganda is to weigh the potential benefits against the potential harm, recognizing that the influence they wield can have far-reaching consequences.

One of the most important ethical considerations in the use of propaganda is the respect for truth. Propaganda often involves distorting or selectively presenting information to achieve a specific outcome. While this may be effective in the short term, the long-term consequences of eroding trust in information can be profound. When people realize they have been misled, their trust in leaders, institutions, and even each other can be permanently damaged. A society where people are skeptical of information and mistrustful of those in power is one that struggles to function cohesively. The responsibility of those who use propaganda is to recognize the value of truth and the importance of maintaining public trust.

Another aspect of the responsibility associated with propaganda is the impact on individuals' autonomy. Propaganda seeks to influence beliefs and behaviors, often by appealing to emotions rather than reason. This manipulation of emotions—such as fear, anger, or pride—can override individuals' ability to think critically and make informed decisions. The ethical responsibility of those who use propaganda is to respect the autonomy of their audience, ensuring that people have the information they need to make their own choices rather than being coerced into a particular viewpoint. The use of propaganda that strips individuals of their ability to think independently is a violation of their rights and dignity.

The creation of enemies through propaganda is another area where the power and responsibility of influence must be carefully considered. The portrayal of a group as an enemy serves to unify the population and justify certain actions, but it also fosters hatred, dehumanization, and division. The responsibility of those who use propaganda is to consider the long-term impact of creating enemies, recognizing that the hatred and prejudice instilled in the population can persist for generations. The power to create an enemy must be wielded with caution, as the consequences of fostering animosity and division are often far more damaging than the initial benefits.

Leaders and media outlets that use propaganda must also consider their role in shaping the values and norms of society. Propaganda has the power to normalize certain behaviors, attitudes, and beliefs. When propaganda promotes prejudice, intolerance, or violence, it contributes to a culture where these behaviors are accepted and even encouraged. The responsibility of those who use propaganda is to consider the kind of society they are helping to create. Are they fostering a culture of empathy, understanding, and cooperation, or are they contributing to division, hatred, and conflict? The power to shape societal values comes with the responsibility to promote a just and inclusive society.

The reflection on the power and responsibility of propaganda ultimately comes down to a question of ethics and intent. The influence that propaganda wields is immense, and those who use it must be mindful of the potential for both positive and negative outcomes. The responsibility lies in ensuring that propaganda is used not to manipulate, deceive, or incite hatred, but to inform, unite, and uplift. The power of propaganda can be harnessed for the common good, but it requires a commitment to truth, transparency, and respect for the rights and dignity of all individuals.

The weight of influence that comes with propaganda is heavy. It is a tool that can bring people together or tear them apart, inspire positive change or sow the seeds of conflict. Those who wield this power must recognize the responsibility they hold—to use their influence ethically, to respect the autonomy and dignity of their audience, and to consider the long-term impact of their actions on society. Propaganda is more than just a means to an end; it is a force that shapes the world we live in, and those who use it have a duty to wield it with care, integrity, and a deep sense of responsibility for the future they are helping to create.

Appendix: Tools for Understanding and Creating Influence

References and Further Reading
The topic of propaganda is vast and multifaceted, with a long history that spans many different cultures, political systems, and contexts. The following references and suggested readings provide an in-depth understanding of the power, techniques, and consequences of propaganda, as well as historical and contemporary case studies that illustrate its use. These resources will help readers explore the subject further, providing insights into both the positive and negative applications of propaganda throughout history.

1. **"Propaganda: The Formation of Men's Attitudes" by Jacques Ellul**
   A foundational text on the study of propaganda, Ellul's work delves into the mechanisms through which propaganda shapes public opinion and the conditions that make people susceptible to it. It provides a comprehensive analysis of propaganda techniques and their psychological impact on individuals.
2. **"Manufacturing Consent: The Political Economy of the Mass Media" by Edward S. Herman and Noam Chomsky**
   This book explores how mass media serves as a propaganda tool for political and economic elites, shaping public perception through the manipulation of information. It is a crucial resource for understanding how modern propaganda

operates in democratic societies.

3. **"The Art of War" by Sun Tzu**
   Though not explicitly about propaganda, this classic treatise on strategy discusses the importance of deception and psychological warfare—concepts that are foundational to effective propaganda. Sun Tzu's insights into strategic influence are relevant for understanding how to craft impactful messages.

4. **"Propaganda" by Edward Bernays**
   Known as the "father of public relations," Bernays provides an insider perspective on how propaganda is used to influence public opinion and behavior. This book offers insights into the ethical considerations of using propaganda and its role in shaping society.

5. **"The Anatomy of Fascism" by Robert O. Paxton**
   Paxton's exploration of fascist movements provides a clear understanding of how propaganda was used to create enemies, unite the populace, and justify extreme policies. It offers historical context and examples that illustrate the impact of enemy creation through propaganda.

6. **"1984" by George Orwell**
   While a work of fiction, Orwell's dystopian novel provides a powerful exploration of the use of propaganda to control society. The concept of "Big Brother" and the manipulation of information are enduring examples of how propaganda can be used to maintain power.

Suggested Resources for Developing Propaganda Campaigns

For those interested in understanding the process of developing propaganda campaigns—either for academic study or practical application—the following resources provide guidance on strategy, techniques, and the ethical considerations involved.

1. **Books on Marketing and Persuasion**
   Books such as "Influence: The Psychology of Persuasion" by Robert Cialdini and "Made to Stick: Why Some Ideas Survive and Others Die" by Chip Heath and Dan Heath offer insights into how to craft messages that resonate with audiences. While not strictly about propaganda, these works are useful for understanding how to create compelling narratives that influence behavior.
2. **Online Courses on Media and Communication**
   Websites like Coursera, Udemy, and edX offer courses in media strategy, communication, and persuasive writing. Courses such as "Introduction to Marketing" or "The Science of Persuasion" provide a foundation for understanding how to create and disseminate messages that influence public perception.
3. **Handbooks on Strategic Communication**
   "The Strategic Communication Imperative" by James Farwell and "Strategic Influence: Public Diplomacy, Counterpropaganda, and Political Warfare" by J. Michael Waller are useful resources for those looking to understand the intersection of propaganda, public relations, and strategic influence. These books provide practical advice on crafting and delivering messages that shape public perception.
4. **Psychology Textbooks on Behavioral Influence**
   Understanding the psychological principles behind influence and persuasion is key to developing effective propaganda. Textbooks such as "Social Psychology" by David Myers and "The Psychology of Attitude Change and Social Influence" by Philip Zimbardo explore how attitudes are formed, changed, and manipulated—essential knowledge for crafting impactful campaigns.
5. **Documentaries and Case Studies**

Documentaries such as "The Century of the Self" by Adam Curtis and "The Great Hack" by Karim Amer and Jehane Noujaim provide visual case studies of propaganda in action. They offer insights into how messages are crafted and disseminated, and the ethical considerations involved in influencing public perception.

6. **Workshops on Narrative Framing and Messaging**
Workshops and seminars on storytelling, public relations, and crisis communication—often hosted by communication consultancies or media organizations—can provide hands-on experience in crafting narratives. These workshops can help participants understand how to frame issues in ways that resonate with audiences and achieve strategic goals.

7. **Software and Tools for Social Media Campaigns**
Understanding modern propaganda requires familiarity with social media and digital platforms. Tools like Hootsuite, Buffer, and Google Analytics are essential for managing social media campaigns, analyzing audience engagement, and refining messaging strategies. These tools are commonly used by propagandists to spread messages, create viral content, and build narratives that reach large audiences.

Milton Keynes UK
Ingram Content Group UK Ltd.
UKHW032034191024
449814UK00010B/539